kara

anditwasbeautiful

*celebrating life in the midst
of the long good-bye*

David C Cook®

transforming lives together

AND IT WAS BEAUTIFUL
Published by David C Cook
4050 Lee Vance View
Colorado Springs, CO 80918 U.S.A.

David C Cook Distribution Canada
55 Woodslee Avenue, Paris, Ontario, Canada N3L 3E5

David C Cook U.K., Kingsway Communications
Eastbourne, East Sussex BN23 6NT, England

The graphic circle C logo is a registered trademark of David C Cook.

LCCN 2015952885
ISBN 978-0-7814-1352-7
eISBN 978-1-4347-1006-2

© 2016 Kara Tippetts
Published in association with William K. Jensen Literary
Agency, 119 Bampton Court, Eugene, OR 97404

The Team: Ingrid Beck, John Blase, Nick Lee, Helen Macdonald, Susan Murdock
Cover Design: Amy Konyndyk
Background Cover Image: iStockphoto
Cover Photo: Jason Tippetts
Interior Photos: Jen Lints Photography

Printed in the United States of America
First Edition 2016

1 2 3 4 5 6 7 8 9 10

123015

for Jason

Contents

ACT TWO

ACT THREE

ACT FOUR

Introduction

I was here. I saw beauty. I embraced it.

That's what Kara Tippetts said. That's also what she lived in her thirty-nine years. And then she died. Some people might cringe at that last sentence, might say a person that age is just getting started. Such people didn't know Kara Tippetts. Although born with a poet's knack for paying attention, the last few years of her life were laser focused because of the presence of cancer throughout her body, a cancer that she grew to call a "gift."

> Every moment seems so special. The truth is,
> it is. That is the gift of cancer. The struggle

is the fear. The fear of this amazing world of people I love more than anything marching forward without me in it. There is a lot of pride and arrogance in that thinking. A friend and I were talking about the control that comes with thinking life is as it should be with us in it. But the truth is, life is exactly planned. Exactly numbered. My job in this day is to live near to Jesus. To seek faithfulness in this day. I want to have a peaceful heart that embraces each gift of joy as it comes.

Some people might bristle at using the word *gift* to describe cancer. Such people should have met Kara Tippetts. She might not have changed their mind, but she definitely would have caused them to at least consider her perspective. To be in her presence was to be in the presence of someone surrendered to God—not resigned but surrendered, and there is a difference. And that difference was persuasive in the most naturally wooing of ways.

This book is a collection of her writings, most of them taken from her blog, *Mundane Faithfulness*. Care has been taken to present her thoughts with a minimum of changes out of a sense of respect. Kara had a distinct voice and a special way of arranging words; her style continues to draw people months after her death. The entries here are arranged according to "acts" like the acts in a play. The acts do not represent a strict chronology, but they do follow the arc of her story. This approach may seem very basic, but Kara would have approved heartily. She liked the simple and the mundane, believing that it was in the ordinary that she saw the beautiful. And for Kara, the beautiful was

> like a ship
> that carried [her]
> through the wildest storm of all.
> —Rainer Maria Rilke

You will notice three complete acts listed in the table of contents. Kara is living her fourth act now in the presence of the One who kept her on this earth, and keeps her still, now in His loving arms.

You will see the names of Kara's family throughout these chapters. For those of you not familiar with them, they are

Jason (husband), Ella Grace (oldest daughter), Harper Joy (next daughter), Lake Edward (son), and Story Jane (youngest daughter). Also mentioned are her sister (Kara spelled it "seester"), Jonna, and Kara's good friend and caregiver, Mickey.

It is our privilege to publish this book posthumously. Our prayer is that Kara's words bring you encouragement and hope. We know they have and continue to do so for us.

The David C Cook Editorial Team

ACT ONE

My dream went all the way back to the beginning.

—Jonathan Safran Foer, *Extremely Loud and Incredibly Close*

1

Grace Dress

A week ago my dear friend Bill Petro helped me get my new blog up and running. I have since been wondering what my first post would be. All the details of my cancer (well, most of them) have been made public. I have decided to share one particular moment when grace really showed up for me in a meaningful way.

I was undone one day last week by an article that indicated my life expectancy. The article itself was sent in love, but all my simple mind could see was the statistical data for how long I would live. Up until that point, Jason and I had been broken and crying, but so full of peace. That evening I would not sleep, I was sick, and I continually added the number listed to each of my children, and I lost my peace.

Grace showed up the next day in a big, big way. When I woke up, I was in bad shape. I asked my neighbor if she could take Lake for the day, and then a friend called to see if she could bring me dinner. I asked her if she was willing to prepare it at my house and watch Story Jane. She said yes and came right over. I then called a woman I knew who had walked the road I was on. She came at 1 p.m. to take me for a walk. She offered joy in the midst of my pain, and hope for a beautiful story all my own. I felt my peace being restored throughout that time.

I came home exhausted and asked my dear I'm-cooking-you-dinner friend if she minded if I took a nap. She scooted me upstairs and off to bed. I woke up a little later and realized Jen Lints was coming to take our last family pictures where I would have hair. I came downstairs bleary-eyed and wondered aloud what our gang was going to wear for the pictures. My cooking-dinner friend said, "You said you liked my dress, right?" She then walked out to her car to get some extra clothes, came back in, and literally took the dress off her back and gave it to me. That's right, I really have those kinds of friends, friends who will take my children, clean my house, cook my dinner, take our family's picture, take me on encouraging walks, and give me the shirt (or dress) right off their back.

I call that dress my grace dress. I literally wore it for three days in a row after my dear friend gave it to me. I wear it to anything that feels hard. I will be wearing it to my first chemo treatment. Yesterday I cut off all my hair so it won't be as hard for the kids when I lose it. I wore my grace dress. After my haircut I decided to sleep in it. Cutting my hair was not really the hard part. I've had short hair many times in my life. It was why I had to cut it. After cutting it short, my next step will be cutting it bald. Grace will have to show up that day like a comfy gray cotton dress. And I believe it will.

Thank you to all of you who are walking with me, whether up close or from a distance. I feel so very loved. Our family has been embraced, prayed for, and miraculous peace has shown up in very real ways. I know I am not facing cancer alone. I know it.

2

Magic Numbers and Lunch Boxes

It's 1:45 a.m. and I am .2 of a degree from needing to go to the hospital. They gave us this magic number and if we reach it, then we fly to the hospital. I can't take drugs to bring down the fever, so I simply have to wait. The past few days have been miserable with small glimpses of lovely.

My kids are adjusting to coming to my bedside for some quality time with me. I have found them watching me sleep. I'm not sure what is playing in their minds, but I see love in their eyes. I wake to my nightstand covered in scrap paper letters of love that bring me strength.

I'm not doing anything fantastic. I'm just trying to live well. Before chemo, living well was easy, effortless. I had freedom to move, hike, snuggle, and keep pace however I chose. Now, I'm sidelined, and feeling bad. When I first found out I was sick, I begged people to pray that I would be kind in my sickness. I don't believe illness gives you a pass to be unkind. It's a tall order and a grace challenge indeed.

The hardest part has been with the kids. I am sad because I want to be intricately involved in the heart matters of my children. I feel sidelined and confused. I am daily being stripped of my idols of self, strength, and independence. It's painful, and it's good. I'm not sure how this cancer is going to change all of us, but change us all it will. Tonight I'm simply praying we stay .2 below that magic number so my babies won't wake up to their mama in the hospital.

No amount of preparation readies a person for the realities of cancer. Jason and I truly loved the ignorance and bliss of the unknown. An old friend sent a detailed email with tips, ideas, and help to face the coming battle we are about to enter. I perused it, then forwarded it to

Jason. By the time the chemo day hit, I had that email memorized. But even then I wasn't ready for the horrible tastes, dry mouth, joint pain, nausea. I still don't want to admit that I'm really sick. Wasn't I just out running the other day? Wasn't I healthy?

When I feel a glimmer of strength, I run downstairs to be with the kids. They flock for hugs and back scratches. Cancer wants to be a thief and steal my moments, but there is always grace. There is always room for Jesus and love. I feel like I'm coming out of a three-day cloud into a lighter misty fog. I am told the clouds will clear just in time for my next chemo treatment.

I had this one task that was gnawing at me to get done before school started. I wanted to buy the kids new lunch boxes. Our current ones are on their last legs, and I had in mind that a "good mama" would replace them. Trivial, I know, but I'm committed. I had just a sliver of energy today, so Jason honored my request and we went to buy lunch boxes.

The kids were tickled with them, and I'm thankful to have been able to do this one thing for them. A friend did their school supply shopping, and another friend took care of back-to-school clothes shopping while I was in my fog. I feel so blessed by this help, but I also felt blessed by the ability to do the lunch box thing. I pray for the energy this coming year to help the kids make lunches to put in those lunch boxes. I pray for that.

3

The Cost of the Cure

You're sitting in your backyard one afternoon and suddenly you start losing your hair, one handful at a time. There's nothing that can prepare you for that moment. But there we were, Story Jane and me, pulling out handfuls of my hair. I thought of Sarah, Plain and Tall giving the hair from a haircut to the fields for the birds to build nests. I would love to see nests of hair like mine. No, actually I wouldn't. I would rather keep my hair.

It is both weird and creepy to have your hair come out in handfuls. It is as though my hair has just quit on me. On the bright side, my breast cancer lump is getting noticeably smaller. So I stomach the bad with the good. All vanity aside, I want to live. And if losing my hair means I can be present for another snuggle, another spelling test, another packed lunch, another load of laundry, another prayer, another shared coffee with Jason, another bike ride, another morning worship, another giggle over a body function, another chance to cry, another meal with friends on the back porch, another camping trip, and another moment praising my Savior, then so be it. This loss of hair is worth another tomorrow. I trust that Jesus knows exactly how many more tomorrows I have. He knows exactly every hair that's coming out by the handful today.

So the next time you see me, I may be sporting a hat or a wig, maybe even a scarf. Whatever reality soon finds me, I pray it finds me in perfect peace with the One who holds my yesterday, today, and tomorrows.

> Preserve me, O God, for in you I take
> refuge....
>
> You make known to me the path of life;
> in your presence there is fullness of joy;
> at your right hand are pleasures
> forevermore. (Ps. 16:1, 11)

4

Big Day

Kids are so honest. Yesterday was a big day for me. My first day in public sporting my new Sinéad O'Connor look, my first day wig shopping, and the first time one of my kids asked if I was going to die. I'd call that big, wouldn't you?

I walked in from wig shopping and Harper Joy asked me if I was going to die. I looked at her and said, "Yes." Then I invited her upstairs with me as I put on comfy clothes. Big conversations require an elastic waist. We jumped on my bed for an honest conversation. I first wanted to know why she asked me that question. She said she was swinging on the playground and a friend said to her, "I sure hope your mom doesn't die." Up until that moment, I don't think she'd considered it. Up until that moment, she had only enjoyed the fruits of cancer: lots of people and lots of love.

This was a special moment for Harper and me. I spoke honestly that I would die, that she would die, that death is a reality for us all. I asked if she knew where I would go when I die. She said, "Mommy, you will go to be with Jesus in heaven." I asked her if I did anything to deserve that and she said, "No." I told her how Jesus in His goodness placed His love on me, and that Christ paid it all for me and for her. We talked about cancer being very scary. I told her the doctor has a good plan, but only God knows how long I will live. I told her it was okay to be sad. Then my sweet Harper Joy cried. And so did I.

I wish I could take away the fears of this sweet, tender-hearted little girl. But I can't. I encouraged her to talk to the One who cares for her every breath. Even though it hurts to watch your children suffer, I know He has plans for her good through this suffering. There are a lot of hard parts to this, but that is probably the hardest. The kids are trying to be positive and brave, but every day I look less and less of what they've known me to be. So we're all doing the best we can, trusting that Scripture means what it says, that God's grace is sufficient. That God's grace is enough.

5
Hard Hard

I am just beginning to surface from my second chemo treatment. I've found a bottom that I didn't know existed. I can typically muscle through, tough it out, but I can't shake the discouragement that this treatment has brought on tonight. As for care, I have the best. But I'm so discouraged, so weary.

I despair at the thought of having to do this four more times and feeling worse with each treatment. My days are measured by how many hours I can sit in a chair instead of being in the bed, by the decreasing numbers of pills I need to make it through the day, or just by being able to eat again. I'm trying so hard to be well for those who have a desire for me to be well. But my texts recently have been brief—"It's hard."

I see people on Facebook welcoming autumn, and I feel like I'm going to lose it in a haze of drugs and sleep. I remind myself that my doctor said my tumor is shrinking, but it's difficult not to feel like a cure this hard isn't going to hurt me somewhere else. I know a lot of people have done this before me with a lot of grace. My dear friend Anna keeps telling me there will be good days. But there are also bad days, days like today when I need to be reminded of His new-every-morning mercies. Good or bad, she always tells me to look for the gifts, because they're always there. But you've got to look.

Can't we just skip to me being well?

6

My Hero

*The saying is trustworthy: If anyone aspires to
the office of overseer, he desires a noble task....
He must manage his own household well, with
all dignity keeping his children submissive, for if
someone does not know how to manage his own
household, how will he care for God's church?*

1 Timothy 3:1, 4–5

I have lived over fourteen years with my hero. He took
1 Timothy 3 seriously even before we were introduced.
Jason is my daily reminder of grace. I will be very clear—
he's not perfect, but he's humble in his imperfection. He is

not my idol, though I have wrestled with that in my heart. As Beth Moore says, "He makes a fantastic husband, but a lousy savior."

When I look at the verses in 1 Timothy, and then I look at Jason, what I see is God-given gentleness. This quality causes him to lead his family well, to not be quarrelsome. It has certainly kept him the husband of one wife. Being a person who spent years uncertain of love and acceptance, I have lived in the reflection of the gospel as my husband has loved me in my sin, ugly and unlovely. Acceptance with Jason has nothing to do with performance but everything to do with his understanding of how loved he is by God in his own weakness and sin.

Let me tell you of the situation my hero has recently found himself in. After a cross-country move with a large family, his wife lands facedown on a tile floor, only to discover she has a heart condition. Six months later, another stressful move to a new house and then ten days later fleeing said house due to wildfires. While all this is happening, he has a huge ordination exam to prepare for, plus all that's involved with starting a new church. And then he finds his young wife has cancer.

At least once every day I say to him, "I'm sorry your wife has cancer." I really am sad that is the way the Father is refining Jason, but that's our story. This is how God is lovingly leading us. Cancer is the gift (there, I said it) of suffering that is refining us both. It is breaking us of ourselves, and of the illusion of strength. It is causing us to see all things beautiful in the mundane. My hero keeps pointing us all to the One who loves us best. Jason does this in plenty and in want, in sickness and in health, till death do us part.

7

Reasonable, Right?

Do you remember the Bill Murray movie *What about Bob?* There is a scene where Bob is tied to the mast of the sailboat, screaming, "I'm sailing!" I felt like that yesterday. All day I kept thinking, *I'm cleaning! I'm driving! I'm in Target!* I know that sounds ridiculous, and I've certainly had the opportunity to do some of those things along the journey, but with each new day I feel such gratitude for getting past chemo.

When I first heard my diagnosis, one of my biggest fears was how my kids would react to having a sick mama. What I feared was their withdrawal. But this has brought the opposite. I thought they would be afraid of my bald head, but they've actually embraced it, adopting the habit of rubbing and kissing my head. This was God's answer to one of my biggest fears. Thank You, God!

Jason and I go this morning to meet with my breast surgeon to finalize my upcoming surgery and to discuss my options. My particular brand of cancer hasn't left me with a lot of options, but I do have a few decisions to make. People often ask me how I feel facing a double mastectomy. My response is usually the same: "I'm much more open to facing pain than months of chemo-induced nausea." That seems reasonable, right? Easier?

I woke up at 4 a.m. this morning unable to shake my angst over my surgery. Not long ago I met a lovely woman who had just completed her surgery journey. She was gracious to show me what I was facing. Her surgery and reconstruction came out beautifully, but all I remembered were the amount of cuts and the scarring she had. Although I have experienced moments of great peace, there have also been moments of debilitating fear.

8

Ugly Me

I'm not sure why talking with the surgeon the other day was so difficult. It's not as though we heard anything unexpected. It's just that what we heard was tough. It's our next step, a step closer to the end of this journey. But it's a daunting one. Hearing the details of my recovery left us both quiet and sad.

I was feeling so good, and then the other day I was humbled and left discouraged. Here are the things I hear myself saying over and over: "Hard is grace too. Don't imagine yourself in the future, because that is you without the grace provided for that moment. There is peace for this day—find it." And I kinda want to tell myself to shut up.

Aren't I lovely? That's the ugly me. The frustrated, struggling, and not wanting to swallow this big pill me. The not really wanting my kids to see my suffering again me. But what I want is life, and this is the cure, and these are the steps in that direction. So we'll take them and see where they lead.

9

The Innocents

In the midst of my pain, there is more as lives are cut horribly short in Sandy Hook. I cannot imagine the devastation in that small town. We lived in the town next to Littleton when the shooting at Columbine occurred. It was horrific, but in the aftermath we saw a new conversation begin. It was not a call for gun control or mental health services, but more a plea to examine our hearts. To look into eternity and examine what happens after death.

I woke today grieving the children and teachers killed. I'm grieving for the witnesses to that scene, for the officials involved, the coroners doing their job. I'm also grieving for the parents sending their living children back to the school now filled with so many vacancies.

I don't know what to tell my children. I emailed our pastor asking what would be said in Sunday's service. I want this reality to not exist in their childhoods as it didn't exist in mine. But it does. I don't understand this tragedy. I cannot comprehend it. I don't know what to tell my children. I just don't know.

Lord, help us all as we shepherd our young children. Help us know how to love their hearts well today. Help us know how to point them to You, the true Comforter. We are all hurting because of this unthinkable act. Help us to know how You would have us live today. We need You today and every day. O come, O come, Emmanuel! Amen.

10

What Matters

With only two or maybe three brain cells that want to function, it was probably not wise for me to hide the Christmas presents. I keep thinking I need to find them all and remind myself what I purchased. Before my last chemo, I tried to get a lot done. This year has been so hard, I really wanted Christmas to not be a bummer. I'm not sure what I have or where I've hidden it. With four kids, I have secret fears of one having lots to open while another only has a few. Ugh.

One of the things we've learned this crazy year is to enjoy the moments. The thing about suffering is it makes the sweet moments so much sweeter. I know people who only want to sign up for the party, only want to hear the good news. That simply has not been reality, or our reality anyway. The joy in the mundane feels so much more real when sadness has been walked through and tasted.

One evening one of the kids came in our room because of a nightmare. Our practice in such moments is to scoot over, snuggle, and pray with our child. Once he or she has fallen back asleep, Jason transfers them back to their bed. Of course sometimes we all just fall sound asleep and wake up with someone's foot in our face. But on this particular night I was sick and awake, trying to pass the time on Pinterest or TasteSpotting. All at once she began to rub my neck and my head. My first instinct was to tell her to stop and go back to sleep. But as I lay there, I realized a new compassion and love that had grown in her through our difficult year. Even with all the hardships, our children had grown in hospitality and love. They had learned to welcome and love strangers. They had learned flexibility. And they had grown in grace.

I think even if the scales of Christmas morning come out a little unbalanced because of their flighty mom, maybe our kids will have some sense of what suffering has taught us this year. Maybe we'll all be a little more acquainted with kindness in our daily struggles. Maybe that's what really matters. Maybe that's the best gift, the one we really need.

11

Christmas Miracle

At the end of my final chemo treatment, I struggled to stand. I didn't have the strength to hold my body upright. I had lost more weight, and I was ready to tear my port out. I asked my doctor about that and he said, "Never mess with a working IV." My mind had grown weary, and I had little enthusiasm for an end-of-chemo celebration. You end chemo on chemo, if that makes sense. So there's little excitement for feeling terrible. Little energy for getting weaker. I struggled to understand how I might possibly be strong enough to endure a major surgery in three weeks.

My Christmas miracle happened two nights ago. My amazing neighbor and I packed up our babies, popped popcorn and made hot chocolate for the older kids, and went out hunting for excellent Christmas lights. People really go all out around here, so it was such a fun time. Here is where my miracle comes into play. When we got back home, my sweet baby girl had fallen asleep. I was able to pick her up and carry her to bed. I had the strength to not just hold her, but to carry her up a flight of stairs to bed. Just a few short weeks before, I couldn't stand and could barely handle the stairs. But on that night I carried my girl like a mama ought to be able to. That may sound small to you, but to me, it was grand.

I woke Sunday before church paralyzed with the fear that I haven't done enough loving in the midst of my sickness. I was afraid that if my life were to be suddenly taken during surgery, would I leave the cups of my children full? Would they remember the love I had for them? Our pastor, Mark Bates, reminded me of a truth I so often forget: that only His love is sufficient for true life. So the freeing answer to my own fears of not having loved enough is, of course, I haven't. My love will never be enough. But the One who sacrificed Himself on a tree many years ago loves my children far more than I do. I don't need to struggle to wonder if I have loved enough in this life. That's in God's hands.

12

In Review

I love many things, but in 2012 I have loved Jesus, my hunky husband, my kids, my girlfriends, and the many mothers who have cared for my family and me. I love a hot fire in the fireplace, and I stinking love hot wings and anything flavored with buffalo flavoring. The year 2012 was a gift, a wonderful, terrible, tough, gnarly, amazing year.

This year showed us the fragility of life. It caused me to consider how, why, and what I live my life for in the moments at home, in quiet, in public, and in my community. This year brought nearness as well as distance to people I love. With limited strength, I found it hard to maintain relationships. My weakness hurt on so many levels. The year 2012 caused me to consider my actions, my thoughts, and how I desire to spend my energy. Through a fall, a fire, and cancer, this year has given me new eyes with which to see Jesus.

The year 2012 was tough, but a great teacher. I don't hate 2012. I don't hate cancer either. Well, sometimes I do. As much as I long to move on from both of them, I'm thankful for the heart-changing breaking they have been to me. But before I make it sound as if cancer or the year were my teachers, they weren't. It was God in His good and perfect providence to number my days, to count the hairs on my head, to not only plan but join me in my suffering. Jesus is my song. Jesus is my guide. Jesus is my hope.

Driving to Denver, I considered finishing up the details of our will before surgery. Should surgery take me home, I want certain things in order. This was not me surrendering. It was a beautiful moment of me thinking about all the love I know.

We came to this town brokenhearted. We continued to see the grace of brokenness throughout the year. We now have a clearer understanding of the deep brokenness that lives in us all. I have grown more intimate with the only true Comforter for that brokenness. And it has been good.

As this year ends and another begins, I pray I am forever changed by the hard of this year. Part of me wants to sweep the dust off my feet at the doorstep of 2012 and say, "You were not very hospitable." But the truth is I have loved and been loved and known love in so many new ways this year. Certainly four months essentially facedown is not a place I want to revisit. I'm not a glutton for punishment. But I pray I do not squander the lessons of this year. Yes, I am sure that neither death nor life nor anything else in all creation will be able to separate us from the love of God in Christ Jesus our Lord. Amen.

13

An Anxious Heart

I read in Matthew 6:25: "Therefore I tell you, do not be anxious about your life, what you will eat or what you will drink, nor about your body." I believe this, but can I tell you how difficult this is for me right now? At the heart of this passage is this: TRUST. Oh how we love to depend on our own strength. How we like to be rulers of our own destiny. And boy howdy how we like to toot our own horn.

But today these verses are a comfort. I have literally thought, *What will I wear? How will I look?* I walked into a lingerie store before Christmas and walked out in tears. My sister-in-law reminded me I won't be able to lift my arms and clothing is going to be hard after surgery for several weeks. My heart is anxious, and these verses are the medicine I need.

Last night a friend asked me if my heart was ready for Wednesday. Truly I have avoided looking at a calendar. Now that it is less than a week, I cannot avoid it. I have moments of great peace as well as great anxiety. Next Wednesday is my surgery. Jesus has asked me to trust Him. And I do.

14

Head Coverings and Hot Flashes

It didn't take long being in chemo for my body to be pushed into menopause. Lovely hot flashes soon followed. If someone sits behind me in church, they see me bundled up, stripped down, then bundled up again. I'm sure it's as irritating to watch as it is to experience it. But my wigs? Though lovely, they are a vise on my head during a hot flash.

I have two wigs and an endless supply of head coverings. But I'm a simple girl really. I now have a favorite or two and I stick to them, or I go bald. I feel like I've been waiting for my older daughters to get comfortable with my baldness. I wanted them to feel as normal as a kid could with a mama with cancer. I remember the moment Ella finally told me to go bald if that was how I felt the best.

I certainly have moments of feeling extremely self-conscious bald. I have moments when I don't feel that brave sharing my secret. You see, if I were really sick but still had my hair, the world wouldn't know I was sick. But I have started to think that my baldness may encourage or remind someone to do a self–breast exam or make that mammogram appointment they've been putting off for weeks. I get it, that business is uncomfortable. But think of it like this: had my cancer been caught while in my breast and not in my lymph system, I probably could have avoided chemo. That was not the plan for me, but maybe it could be for you.

Soon my hair will return, my breasts will be gone, my cancer will be removed, my hot flashes will remain, and the landscape of my life will look very different. So many people have called me brave. I have never once felt that that word fits. My community and I have just been surviving, facing each moment and looking for the grace to get through it. The ones I find truly brave are the ones who left the comforts of their life to enter into our hard with us. There are those who have stepped into a house of hurting kids, a tired daddy, and a sick mama, and they've offered comfort and hope in our dark season. I'm not brave, but they are.

15

I Made It, But

I made it through the surgery. But it's been a tough recovery. The pain involved has been hard. I have moved from big general pain to sharp local pain. The narcotic fog is lifting and I'm beginning to remember parts of the last couple of days. Sadly, I remember coming out of surgery. They did not have my pain managed when I woke up. I cry thinking about the terror of waking up feeling like I had been stabbed. Plus screaming and vomiting in pain and panicking that Jason would see me in such a state.

It was a hard pill to swallow, hearing that I have yet another step in this journey. My oncologist was confident that we had a complete result with chemo. I saw how cancerous my right breast and lymph nodes were. I should not be surprised to learn I have to have radiation. But after the agonizing months of chemo and now surgery, we sure were hoping for an end to this. Will there ever be an end to all of this? I'm having a hard time imagining myself well.

The report came back today. I have two lymph nodes that still have cancer in them; miniscule amounts, but cancer nonetheless. I really want to quit. I don't want to meet a radiologist. I don't want another doctor on my team. But then I look at my family and because of them (and for them) I will do it all. I want to be there for them. I want to know them on their good days and bad days. I want to enjoy life with my family and community. It's just so hard to be sick for so long. I want to be the one caring for them instead of the other way around. I am weary of receiving. It is more blessed to give than to receive, right? Right?

16

How Did I Get Here?

Today, in a moment of desperation, I decided to try acupuncture to help me with my endless hot flashes. When you're in pain compounded by hot flashes all topped off with discouragement, well, it's easy to despair. So there I was prostrate on a bed, looking at the ceiling, with needles all over my body. I thought of my friend across town recovering from a major surgery to remove a tumor. I wondered about her level of desperation. Then I thought of her sweet spirit, and I knew she was gently and graciously loving those who were caring for her.

I looked at this silly butterfly mobile above my head and wondered, *How did I get here?* I'm thirty-six, bald, missing my breasts, unable to dress myself, and maybe never seeing the end of this terrible disease. I am so tired of myself.

Will I ever be healed?

Will this suffering continue?

What is God wanting me to understand through this hard season?

Will God help me to see Him as good even if my questions are not answered in the way I want them to be?

I prayed these same questions for my friend in bed across town awaiting the pathology results of her tumor. We're both crying out to Jesus that she won't have cancer. But I'm also crying out that we would not doubt His goodness regardless of the results. Those are hard prayers to pray.

The acupuncture doctor felt my pulse and said, "You're weak; your energy is very low." It was all I could do not to be snarky. *Wow, what gave me away? Was it the drain tubes, my bald head, my black eyes, the IV bruises up and down my arm, or my constant wincing in pain?* But I had to remember my own words, how illness is not an excuse to be unkind. So I bit my tongue, hard.

Though I had asked for help taking off my clothes for the appointment, I was too proud to ask for help getting dressed again. After a long time fighting my clothes back on, I left the place of needles, that room of desperation. I called Jason and shared my heavy heart with him. His precious response to my heartbroken tears was, "He promises to be with us, Kara. What we need is His presence no matter the answer."

I still wonder how I got here. But the hope I'm holding on to is that He is here too.

17

Grace Shows Up

I feel like I have two major mantras that have grown out of this year. First, hard is grace too. And second, grace will show up. It always does, but we usually have to look for it.

I woke up yesterday morning both excited and bummed. It was a day I had really been looking forward to for some time. My big seester was flying to town, plus a most favorite author of mine was going to come for a visit. My bummed feeling was due to still having my drain tubes in. Not only are they uncomfortable, but I only have two things I can wear with them. I know that's pure vanity, but I was simply looking forward to meeting someone I so admire for the first time in something other than Wal-Mart sweats.

I was dragging getting ready, very unexcited to face my limited wardrobe, when I heard the door opening. It was my seester, a gift of grace walking through the door. As soon as she walked in, I noticed her dress—the cutest shapeless dress with buttons around the neck. When I realized, *Hey, I could wear that!* I told her I just had to borrow it. Jonna looked at me and said, "You are the ONLY person I would do this for. I just bought this dress!" I love having a sister.

Yes, I had another moment like this when a dear friend took off the dress she was wearing and gave it to me. Something about me and dresses, huh? To repay my sister for her dress kindness, I took her out for Mexican food (which makes everything better).

Jonna's dress was grace #1 that day. Grace #2 was that Sally Lloyd-Jones was coming to my house! Following my surgery, I had quoted her book *The Jesus Storybook Bible* in a blog post. A friend realized that Sally was coming to Focus on the Family, and so he organized a meeting with her, as in I-get-to-meet-her. Spending time with her was like sitting down to a great meal. She was so encouraging and gracious and transparent. The time was like being with an old friend.

I told Sally of the struggles we face and the heartbreaks that have grown us in Jesus. I told her how writing has kept me from feeling so isolated. She told me about her writing process, and her heart's desire to bring joy to children by pointing them to the Author of true joy. I was so comfortable with her, I even told her how I didn't want to meet her in my Wal-Mart sweatpants!

18

Suffering and Sovereignty

Some of my most difficult conversations I have had in the midst of my cancer have been with believers who do not see God in a hard plan. So many believe that hard comes and then God makes it better. It is so easy to forget that our salvation came by way of the hard of a cross. In those conversations, the story that always comes to mind is that of Joseph.

Before Joseph suffered, he dreamed the end of his story. He dreamed the moment his brothers would bow down to him, a moment God ordained to save many in the midst of famine. But what did Joseph have to endure? Rejection, jail, false accusations, misery. Every bit of his hard was part of the plan, and it was all for the glory of God.

I know it's easy, as a Christian, to buy into the American ideal that happiness is the goal, that protection from suffering is really living. Some people have entered our home uncomfortable with how much my children understand my suffering. Sally Lloyd-Jones was such a reassuring treasure to me. We spoke about how people do not give their children enough credit. Jason and I let our children lead the discussion; we let them ask what their hearts are ready to understand.

I see my children struggle when we keep them in the dark and they sense our stress without knowing our hearts. We did not want to tell our children about radiation, that the story of cancer was continuing. The fact is that we didn't want to tell ourselves that either. But once we faced it honestly, something happened. Peace ran through the painful nooks of avoidance. The stress lessened and the grace to face the new hard entered the crevices of unbelief. We are kept, closely kept near to Jesus in the midst of our story.

Back to Joseph. I'm reminded how he suffered, how he was hurt and forsaken by those who were supposed to love and protect him. Through it all he looked to God. There are days when I'm tempted to grow bitter toward those who have forsaken us in this dark season. But like Joseph, I look to God and offer forgiveness and grace to those who bring harm instead of protection. I encourage you to read this story in Genesis, and hopefully see why it brings me such comfort. You see, I believe suffering is caught up in the sovereignty of God. I can't not believe that. Jesus was, after all, the Man of Sorrows, well acquainted with grief.

19

Insignificant Update and Selfish Desires

My hair is returning! Seriously, I need to shave, but I'm just so tickled to be growing hair! My head is full of fuzz! I went to church yesterday and greeted my friends by tilting my head down. Everyone wanted to pet me. I get that.

I was so tired of looking like a thumb. Yes, that's what I thought when I looked in the morning mirror: "Good morning, thumb. You look very strange." But I'm not thumby anymore—I'M GETTING HAIR!

Plus a few selfishly honest words about my loves:

Ella Grace, how could not being here for her gentle heart be better? How will someone else read her heavy heart and know when to push to help her share her heavy burdens? Who else will help her when words refuse to work and her stutter becomes unbearable? Who else, Lord? I so want to see what You have in store for my firstborn.

Harper Joy, how could I not be here to love this giver of love? Who will know her use of silly to protect her heart? This lover of humanity understands my great joy in sharing life with others. Can't we grow old learning the love of others together? And how could I not be here to see the beautifully unique girl grow into a woman?

Lake Edward, oh my only son, my lover of work, my fierce protector, my driven, stubborn, focused son. The Lord has allowed me to be his gentle place, his soft place of

love driven by all those lovely character-
istics. Oh how I want to be the only one
who knows this place until he meets his
forever wife. Lord, wouldn't it be gain for
me to see the wonderful plan You have for
my son?

Story Jane, from the start this one has
brought me the greatest doubt, greatest heartbreak, largest angst. My heart's
struggle is that this one will have to learn
so much of her mama from her daddy
and siblings. When we did not know my
prognosis, I simply could not understand
how heaven would benefit from me being
absent from the eyes of her sweet face. I
want a front-row seat to what God will
grow in this unique heart.

20

Poem for Jason's Birthday

Let's run away today.
How about we hike the South Route,
Sit and read our books on a
blanket in the Glen.
We can do laundry at Stoners,
Let's do lunch at La Casita.
I'll get a bean burrito and you can get
Cheese and chicken enchiladas.
Let's walk the beach in California,
And ride your long board
on the boardwalk.
Again, Mexican food sounds right.

And who needs to be a tourist
When we can talk for endless hours.
How about we have coffee at Encore
And run over to the farmer's market.
Pesto pizza, pesto pasta, pesto all day.
Let's move to Colorado.
How about a walk up Clear
Creek, the library,
Table Mountain Inn for lunch.
Let's have a baby.
Asheville sounds good, the Blue Ridge,
Blue Moon Coffee, Doc
Chey's, another baby.
Let's sneak away to the beach.
Why don't we walk the
Old streets of Charleston. Let's
eat the southern fare
And swim through the humidity.
How about we move down the mountain.
Why don't we eat with Lois and Kenny.
How about we go on a date
with Jerry and Darnell?

Sit on the porch with Skip and Autumn.

Have a backyard fire with

Chad and Nicole.

Let's have another baby!

For your birthday let's run

away to Nashville

And enjoy the love of a sister and brother

and countless nieces and nephews.

Let's eat barbecue and drink more coffee.

How about another baby? Why not!

Why don't we run away to Hilton Head,

We will take turns playing in the

water and tending the babies.

We will enjoy too much food, and

Long walks on the beach cut

short by a tired child.

Why don't you move me back

to the place it all started?

La Casita with kids, the Crags with kids,

Ute Valley Park with kids, fires at night,

Coffee, snuggles, books, kids' books.

Let's pretend that today isn't surgery.

Let's pretend Thursday isn't coming.
Let's run away today and celebrate you.
Let's coffee together, shower together,
Enjoy a fire together, enjoy
Mexican food together.
Let's read a book, talk about
our favorite parts.
Let's drop the kids off at school
with prayers and kisses.
Let's do a dance party and cook
something yummy together.
Happy birthday, Boyfriend, Best friend,
Partner in crime, All-time favorite!
I never for one solitary second
deserved your love,
But I'm so very thankful for it.
Let's go to surgery but spend
the day daydreaming
About the glorious life behind
us, and the wonderful life
Ahead of us! 1-4-3! You have
Given me a lifetime of stanzas! I love you!

21

Heading Out

I got to hear Richard Pratt this morning. He spoke on the Lord's Prayer, and it deeply encouraged my heart. Richard said that if we have been bought by Jesus, then our lives are not our own. I get to love in a new way, I get to share my life in a new way, I get to participate in living while I'm still alive in a new way. My moments are not my own for safekeeping. His message was very convicting and inspiring.

We only have one more week at Village Seven Presbyterian Church before we move out on our own as a new church. Jason woke up this morning well rested, peaceful, and encouraged. He proudly showed me the order of worship bulletin he's been working on for weeks. We are so humbled by what

God has grown in the hearts of our community. We still have a lot of growing to do, bumps to hit, and I'm sure hard days, but doing life together is exciting. It will be hard to leave the safety net of our mother church, but she has nurtured us well, and it's time to go.

When the pathology report from my surgery came back with more cancer, and likely more treatment, the church graciously offered us more time before we start. But Jason and I knew we didn't need it. We are ready to go. Suffering won't take a vacation because we are busy. Besides, God goes before us.

22

Dear Snow Day …

Thank you for showing up just in time. I needed a slow down, sit by the fire, rest and contemplate day. I needed a day of snuggles with my children. I needed your beauty all white and showy. I needed you like I need air.

This week of hearing the amazing Richard Pratt speak, I needed time to digest his brand of courage and life. I longed for a moment when his words could sink deeply into my heart and change me from within, forever. It was good to wrestle through his life-giving, life-challenging, life-invigorating wisdom and prayers for our denomination, and to consider how Jason and I would hear Jesus and His call in a new way. Here, less than two weeks before the church plant begins, his words were a meal we didn't realize we needed.

Lastly, dear Snow Day, thank you for the amazing sledding hill so close to our house. Thank you for its amazingness, thank you that there is no need to bail out. Thank you for neighbors who will watch over my kids as I prepare a warm meal for them to come home to. Sledding hill, you and I will one day meet, but I need more than a week past my latest surgery before I rise to your challenge. But mark my words, I will.

23

The Cancer

Last week our friends from Denver came down for dinner. While my friend and I were cooking, the kids were playing and the boys passed through the kitchen. Their little boy looked squarely at me and said, "Are you done with the cancer yet?" I wasn't sure what he said and he's so darn cute, so I asked him to repeat it. Sure enough—"Are you done with the cancer yet?"

I didn't know quite how to answer him. Certainly I wanted to say, "Yes, sweet boy, I'm done! Thank you for asking." But I couldn't. So I stammered through some kind of a response. His question came from a caring, honest place. But I still struggled with an answer.

My dear friend whom I have walked this road with got a complete result from chemo. That means all her pathology results came back without any cancer remaining. Praise God! And even though her road is far from over, that is just the best news. But that is not my news. They found cancer in the lymph nodes they took out. So I could be cancer-free, but it's not definitive. I may still have it—"the cancer."

24

Divided Mind

Great multitudes followed him, and he healed them all.

Matthew 12:15 KJV

This was the verse yesterday in Spurgeon's *Morning by Morning*. He spoke of the power of God to heal, but God shows His power ultimately in healing our souls. The imputing of peace to those He knows is the healing our hearts truly need. I wholeheartedly believe this, but I daily struggle to take hold of this truth. Today I want healing of my body, like the great multitudes that pressed upon Jesus for the healing of their wounds, diseases, and misery. Like them, I want comfort this moment, this day, this week for my tired little body. I can easily forget the amazing work of healing to my spirit that has already happened. It's in this place that I struggle. I don't want to list one thousand gifts. I simply want the end of this chapter. I want it to stop.

This road is wearisome and long. Medical bills pile on top of medical bills; fear sneaks into uninvited places. With spring approaching, I would normally be filling Jason's in-box with dreams of raised vegetable beds, chicken houses, and playhouses. But for today it was a made bed, a load of laundry started, and walking dirty dishes to the kitchen. That's not a lot, but it's more than the sum total of yesterday.

Yesterday I had one task. One. It was to make scones with Ella for her country report. I could not do it. I just could not. In tears, I asked Jason to call our precious British friend and ask for help. This friend and her sweet daughters not only baked thirty-five scones, but then she delivered them warm to my house with cream and jam. Then another friend showed up with dinner and a smile. I'd have to be blind not to see the grace there. I was so thankful for this, but my gratitude was mixed for I just had one task, one, and I couldn't complete it.

It's days like yesterday when I live with a divided mind—so very thankful, but also so very much wanting things to be different than they are. I wanted to make scones with Ella. I would have loved to prepare dinner for a friend and deliver it. But that was yesterday. Now is today, and my washing machine just stopped, and I have the strength to change out the clothes. And I am grateful to be able to do this one thing.

25

Limping

Monday is the beginning of the end. It is the last week of school and the last week of treatment, at least for now. We are dragging, limping, struggling toward the finish line. When the mama, the go-to cheerleader, the organize-and-keep-it-in-order person is down for the count, everyone suffers. We have had victories, but I must say we barely made it. This year my kids earned grades that will never be quantified on a report card.

Last week I asked if I could have people join me at my last radiation treatment as I ring the bell to mark the end of this journey. I told them I wanted my kids to see me do that. One sweet woman offered to show them the room where I receive treatment. I looked at her soberly and said, "I never want my kids to see the inside of that room. Radiation is a place only for patients, and my constant prayer is that they would NEVER know cancer."

The plaque in the hallway that holds "the bell" has a saying on it:

Ring this bell
three times well,
the toll to clearly say ...
my treatments done,
this course is run,
and I am on my way!

Before I rang that bell, I cried with gratitude for those who have loved us so well. So many were there that day cheering me on in the ringing, the marking of a finish, at least for now. I love Team Tippetts! And you can bet I rang the snot out of that bell, three times well.

ACT TWO

The middle path makes me wary.... But in the middle of my life, I am coming to see the middle path as a walk with wisdom where conversations of complexity can be found, that the middle path is the path of movement.

—Terry Tempest Williams, *Leap*

26

Mickey

One cannot know how they will face cancer. The sick nights and long days in anguish fighting for a good attitude. The stupor of drugs and pain is exhaustingly long. When we started this journey, we knew we needed help to navigate this minefield. We knew we needed the kids to be supported in a gentle, loving way. We knew this was going to break us all.

I have known Mickey since I was seventeen years old. I was a hurting, broken, confused teen and new to my faith. The minute I met her and her children, I knew I wanted to be in her life. To know Mickey is to know you are invited and welcomed. I remember in college struggling with something and

Mickey caught wind of it. She drove down to Bloomington and took me camping. That's Mickey.

When I started treatment, Mickey was in the thick of wedding planning and preparation for her daughter. We told her we wanted her to come, but we knew her schedule was full. In fact, it was overfull. I will never forget when she texted us back: "Give me two weeks to recover, then I'll come stay." That was so humbling. She came before my third treatment, and it was the perfect time. She came in with gentle joy and told us she'd do anything except discipline our children. We said, "Deal."

Through radiation I thought I could tough it. I was tired and in pain, but it was manageable. The person I was missing, though, was Jason. He kept suggesting we call in some help, but I was stubborn, trying to be a tough girl. I was missing my husband's absolute exhaustion. But once I saw this, I suggested he call Mickey, and Jason made the call. We were hoping she would agree to a week; she gave us three. What an absolute gift she has been.

I wish she didn't have to leave. Mickey has helped us see the joy in our days. She has pointed us to kindness with our children. She's helped us say yes more to the requests of our young tween. She has cleaned the kitchen at least a thousand times, thrown a party, welcomed other young mothers into her fold, laughed when our kids chose chips and dip for breakfast and cereal for dinner. Mickey has shown us where the battle was and where the battle wasn't. We could not have done it without her.

You know that verse about entertaining angels unawares? Yes. Mickey.

27

The Worried Well

From the beginning of this journey, it has been made clear to me that moving forward after cancer can be difficult. Today my doctor talked to me about "the sick and the worried well." From the start I didn't want to be the worried well. I wanted to be DONE! I wanted my life back, my old normal life. I wanted emotional drains DONE! Fear? DONE! Cancer? GONE!

When I finished radiation, a nurse sat me down to discuss going forward. She concluded by telling me to do a breast exam. What?! I got rid of those. Didn't I go through excruciating surgery to not have to worry about that again? Well, no. So I complied. And I found an angry lymph node.

I tried to ignore it, kind of like you ignore a bruise that is so satisfying to poke over and over and over. I told Jason. I decided to wait until our vacation was over to give it attention. I didn't want to tell anyone because I'm sick of my never-ending story.

But I made an appointment with my trusty oncologist to get it checked. The doctor took one look at me and said my entire system is angry from radiation. He said I'm so badly burned right now that my lymphatic system is on red alert. He will keep an eye on things, and he's confident it will calm down as my burned skin calms down.

Jason and I drove home in silence. Tired silence. I realized I had not eaten, that plus the anxiety of it all and taking blood, I felt completely tanked. I thought I could do survivorship. But I found out I cannot do "the worried well" on my own. I can't tough it out. So I guess I'll have to keep on being needy, dependent, spent, always begging for grace. It's not a bad place to be, by any means. I'm just tired of it. I just don't want to be sick anymore.

28

Cast Your Cares

We are currently at the one-year mark of the Waldo Canyon fire. That means we're also at the one-year mark of finding my cancer. It's a hard year to reflect on, but it has been a year of seeing God in His faithfulness in a totally new way. If at any point in the year I doubted His faithfulness to me, there was always a reminder of His goodness. Always.

God has also been faithful to my pastor, who is also my husband. For years, as I listened to Jason, I would often think of people his words might encourage. There were also times when I thought who his words might offend. I spent so much energy wanting to be well liked, wanting God to use the words Jason spoke for His glory. If I'm honest, I wanted Jason to succeed, I wanted us to succeed. But something has changed for me this past year. God has untied me from those knots. He has blessed me with a new freedom from worrying or striving. I have happily repented of my desire to please others. And I'm entrusting Jason to God's hands. Isn't that big of me? I know how much he is clinging to Jesus right now, and that intimacy is revealed in the words he shares, be it a sermon or something less structured. Jason has a desperate need to know Jesus and tell others about Him. And that desperation is inviting to others. I can see it. I can hear it. I know it.

29

Choosing a Mentor

Apart from the Holy Spirit, it has been the mentors in my life who have made the longest-lasting, deepest impact on who I am as a person. Some mentors were women I specifically asked to mentor me. Some were women who opened their lives wide open for me to watch. But both nurtured new strength in me. Here are a few things that have served me well in finding a mentor.

First, do they love their family well and speak with love and admiration of their husbands? Can these be areas of tension and struggle in a family? Yes, but I look to see if their overall desire is to move toward a spouse and children, and not away.

Second, do they speak vulnerably about weakness, or are they more concerned about appearances? I have found this area to be critical. I struggle to share openly with someone who wants to appear they have it all figured out. I look to see if they are willing to speak openly about where God is challenging them, and are open about themselves without bashing others.

Third, and most important, do they seek Jesus in their moments throughout the day, especially the mundane? Do they see their neediness and weakness, and are they able to be wrong and be corrected by Scripture?

When Jason was a youth director, we had the privilege of seeing kids who truly loved Jesus. From that observation, we often sought out their parents. We wanted to sit at their feet, eat at their table, and watch how they did it. I love to watch someone discipline with kindness. I love to watch someone including their children in the events of the home. I love watching someone loving their spouse creatively. And I really love to see women involved in community building. You can receive a lot of mentoring just by watching.

Common interests help as well. I have had mamas show me a craft, women who love to write as well as read, ladies who love to garden, build a fire, and cook, and women who just cannot get enough of their Bibles. I often try to enter the life of a person who might be a good fit as a mentor in a place of common joy. I want my mentors to be my friends, as I want to befriend the women I mentor.

Things to be wary of? Be careful of people who like to gossip. Be willing to be flexible. Mentoring relationships take on so many different looks. Sitting down across from one another with Bibles open every week? That's an awesome model, but it's certainly not the only one. Look for someone who will promote freedom in Christ, not tie you up in a load of legalism.

Finally, as you search for a safe place, be a safe place in return. God loves seeing us seeking Him together.

30

Eagle Lake Camp

Yesterday was a big day in the life of our family. It was the first time we sent our girls to summer camp at Eagle Lake. The kids have grown up hearing about the adventures Jason and I shared at Eagle Lake, and now it's their turn. I'd sent Ella to camp before, and I remember the mama anxiety around relationships, safety, homesickness. I worried over every detail of her packing. I worried like it was my job.

Cancer has completely changed my perspective. Unbelievably changed my perspective! Now, when I see an opportunity for life, growth, and adventure, I shove my kids at it. I do make sure things are safe, but then I let them go. As the girls peppered me with questions about my camp experience, I only grew more excited for them. Ella was raring to go. Harper had moments of feeling timid. But yesterday finally came.

It does help that they're going with a gaggle of friends. They will be growing in their faith with people they will come home and do life with next year. Knowing what a tough year the girls have experienced, I can hardly wait for them to have a week of exhausting, exhilarating joy. I pulled the girls aside before we left and explained to them that this is their "safe week." It's their week to share their story, their week to separate from our faith and take hold of their own. I explained how we are not a family that hides behind secrets and that I wanted them to share honestly how this year has been for them. Or if they chose not to talk about it, they had that freedom as well.

I woke up this morning praying for the girls. Praying for their relationships and safety. A big smile grew across my face as I remembered what they would likely be doing this morning. I admit I also prayed the food has improved a bit. Actually a lot.

31

Always Move Toward

Jason and I are very simple in our practices when it comes to parenting. Through the little years, we lived with a basic philosophy: love is kind. That has been the filter through which we look at all of our parenting. If love is kind, then discipline is kind. If love is kind, then even at our most irritated we don't have permission to leave the realm of kindness. This is definitely no small feat, no easy thing to accomplish. But it has served us well. Those three simple words have marked our young years raising children and loving one another. When we have gone outside the boundaries of kindness, it has been our humble opportunity to apologize and ask for forgiveness.

Now our children are getting older and the struggles they face are more complex. The principle of kindness will never be outgrown by any of us in this house. But I have a new extension of that, simply a variation on the theme of kindness: always move toward. The best picture I have of this is that of Jesus continually moving toward me. His face is always toward me, always gently pursuing, always desiring nearness. Even when I turn away, act out, or move toward my own ends, He stays ever focused on moving toward me, not away.

And while this has been my approach to the kids, it has spilled over into my relationship with Jason. My heart's desire is to always be moving toward those people in my life I love so very much. I will fight against the distance, always.

32

When Helping Helps

There is a haze that one enters when one is first diagnosed with cancer. I call it "the grace fog." I believe God was gracious to let us enter into a kind of stupor where we lived from one moment to the next. So many offers for help come in right at the start, but truly, our heads were spinning. There was no way we could clearly articulate our needs. All we really knew was we were broken and needy.

It really took us weeks to understand what we needed. During this time many people just did what they sensed they needed to do. One friend brought fruit often; another brought flowers and placed them throughout our house. One friend brought me beautiful Burt's Bees lotions; another spent hours rubbing my feet (a wonderful distraction from nausea). I never asked for these things, but these friends took the initiative and loved us sweetly in these ways.

After hours of discussing with Jason, we arrived at these thoughts. First, our main concern was the kids. We wanted their hearts gently cared for in our home. We didn't want the older children to grow bitter by being asked to do too much, and we wanted the needs of our little ones to be carefully attended to in our home. So Jason and I prayed through a list of people we felt would love our children well through this difficult time. And in a totally new direction for us, we decided to ask/invite people to live with us.

With someone living here, Jason felt he could continue working. Plus, the kids would have a sense that the house was still functioning as it needed to, even with the mama down. Those first days in and around chemo were the critical ones. I could often be down for the count for five to seven days, so the people we asked to help us REALLY helped us. At the end of their stint, they all left physically exhausted. I'm sure the emotional drain was there too. Countless times the person would fall fast asleep as Jason took them back to the airport.

We also identified local families that were safe for our kids. I had chemo on Wednesdays and typically Fridays were my worst days. We tried hard to have our older girls go to a sleepover that night. We didn't want them to see me in such bad shape. We are a very open family, but even open families can practice discretion at times.

However, there are always those things the kids only want Mama and Daddy to do. Those things, in our house, were bedtime and discipline. Jason is the master of bedtime, so that was easy. Discipline was a little harder. I'd describe it as a dance, and not an easy one to be sure. But it was important that it come from Jason and me. I remember when Mickey first came, she said, "Kara, I don't care how sick you are, you will be doing the discipline. I'm here to bring the love."

I'll try to articulate this. If you have the opportunity to love a sick family, please don't be shocked by bad behavior on the part of the kids. Push into that behavior and love them creatively when you see the ugly sides of their day. The kids are hurting, and they've not developed the communication skills to process all that's going on. It's hard for us as adults to try to talk about these things. Try hard not to expect adult things from those who are still so very young.

In the absence of me, our kids have been loved and mothered by so many. I remember a Moms & Muffins event scheduled for Lake's class. It was to take place two days after my chemo. I couldn't do it, and I cried that I couldn't do it. I cry now thinking of it. My seester had come to town and so Lake invited her to go in my place. That was such a gift to Lake, and to me. I'll never be able to repay her for that. I simply said, "Thank you."

After a year of people coming in and out of our house, our children have learned to welcome all kinds of new people into their lives. I've seen an openness develop in the kids that a year ago was not there. And that's the goal, isn't it, to keep an open heart? I never in a million years would have wished for my kids to have to learn that lesson in this way, but that is some of the beautiful fruit of the ugly. And it is truly beautiful.

33

Life without a Bucket List

I can confidently say that I don't live with a long list of things I want to do, see, or complete before I'm done in this place. I carried a dream for years of having a farm. I was in love with all things Wendell Berry. I could picture it, the life of routine created by the land and its rhythms. But beyond that I've never longed for having a list and checking things off. I'm happy with my old cars, my simple wardrobe, my lack of fancy things and vacations. Don't get me wrong, I do love a good concert, but I also love an organic dance party in my kitchen. I love great food, but I also love a hot dog over the fire pit in my backyard. I love a hike in the mountains, but I also love a walk around the block with my people.

Last week, when I heard I may have another long road to travel on this journey, I turned to Jason and cried. I told him how day after day this place is losing its grip on me. Driving down the street, this place sometimes feels so slutty, so wanting my money without a care for my heart. Billboards blare at me what to buy, what to think, how to vote. But the tie that binds me here is relationships. Sickness makes those bonds more real, more important. It's people who grip my heart.

Suffering has a way of exposing our theology, certainly our practical theology, where what we believe about God collides with where we live. My heart always hurts a little when someone hears my story and begins to question God's goodness. I have found that suffering makes my faith more childlike, more simple. Our ideas of God are not necessarily made bigger or more grandiose through suffering, but they are simplified as we wade through the unknown of what comes next. Last week, in that unknown, I was smooching on Lake and the thought hit me that I won't be around to help him navigate his first heartbreak. I was in a public place and I nearly lost my footing because of the fear that gripped me in that moment. I looked up and saw my growing girls and was almost suffocated by the thought of who will help them during the awkward years of puberty. Shouldn't it be me? That's the way it's supposed to be, right? Can't I stay and be here for them when they need me?

The truth is none of us know the length of our lives. So we pray for daily bread and say thank you when it comes. For today I have a little boy who will cross the room to give me a hug. I have a baby girl who gives me ten kisses when I ask for five. I have a preteen who still holds my hand in public, in front of her friends even. I have a second born who loves to tell me every tiny detail of her day. I have a guy who makes coffee just like I like it. A bucket list? No, I don't need one. I'm so rich. It's relationships that matter. And for me, paying attention to the precious gift of today is the only thing on my list.

34

Indicated, Not Conclusive

I think it surprises people that I'm out, up, and functioning. There is a part of me that wants to hibernate and have someone wake me when it's all done. But life with children doesn't afford that liberty and freedom. Even without children, I don't think we have the freedom to stop. We certainly have the freedom to pause to grieve, to hurt, but a complete stop? No.

As much as I can be in the game, I want to be in it. Present. Living. Today I hear the results of my PET scan. It's a test that indicates where cancer might be hiding out in my body. There are friends and family around the country tied up in knots waiting to hear. Jason wanted to stay home today, but I felt strong enough to face it alone with the kids, and mountains and mountains of laundry.

The PET scan indicated the presence of cancer, emphasis on the word "indicated." That does not mean conclusive. I have met many survivors who have had positives and it turned out it wasn't cancer. It will not be until my hysterectomy next Monday that we will know for certain. We've told all our kids about the surgery, but only Ella knows of the possibility of cancer. I've never wanted some ugly old fibroids more in my life.

35

Dear Uterus …

I want to thank you for Ella, and Harper, and Lake, and Story. You know my heart and how I would have partnered with you to bring many more beautiful faces into this family. Sadly, we are parting ways. I am beyond grateful for your role in my life. These four treasures are such a blessing to me.

Thank you, beautiful womb. I think you are simply miraculous. I think you should be more highly regarded. Dear Uterus, this mama loves what you safely delivered into my arms. But cancer, the cancer, says our journey has come to an end. My heart is grieved. But how can I look at these sweet faces I am blessed with and be that sad? That's right, I can't. So while

parting is a sorrow, it is one of those sweet sorrows, one mixed
with what is and what might have been.

I would write more, but after all, you are a uterus.

Forever grateful,

Kara

36
No Stage Five

A week ago Jason told me about a dream I had in the middle of the night. He said I sat up in bed and had my hands raised, yelling, "The walls are falling in! The walls are falling in!" He told me he held my hand and said, "I've got the walls, babe. I've got them." I keep coming back to that dream today, for that's how I feel.

I remember waking from surgery and continually asking every nurse, "What was my tumor?" I kept asking, and they kept avoiding my question. I know they were trying to keep me calm and comfortable, but I was so agitated at not knowing. They finally wheeled me to my room. On the way there I saw Jason. I gave him no greeting, no sweet words of love, only, "What is it?" He looked soberly at me and told me it was breast cancer. I turned my head and wept. My oncologist had made it clear that this would be the worst possible outcome. The worst.

I am now facing stage-four metastatic cancer. There is no stage five. My oncologist came by, but he offered few options for me. Although people around me clung to his options as hope, I could see through his words. When I mentioned I might take a different path to enjoy living instead of the pain of fighting, my compassionate oncologist looked at me with understanding eyes. It is very clear that what I have is aggressive. It did not take its time working through my tired body.

Jason and I have had moments of crying alone and crying together. There is a lot we cannot comprehend right now. I've been in such a stupor of medication, I haven't fully swallowed this new news yet. I have upset a few people with my blunt assessment of the situation. My options are limited, highly limited. But I'm not without hope. I may lack much hope for my time in this place, but I certainly have not lost hope. I may be dying, but I don't want to be treated like the walking dead. I want to laugh, find joy, fight for my moments. I'm not giving up, but I plan to fight for a life that feels like living.

There certainly are moments like I experienced in my dream, moments when the walls feel like they are caving in on us. But God has been so gracious in directing and loving us well so far. We will trust in the Lord with all our heart, and not lean on our own understanding.

37

Me

Simple title, huh? I'm awake late at night with a desire to tell you more about me. I want to tell about the me that has nothing to do with cancer. I want to tell you a few snippets of me apart from the battle I'm facing. So here we go.

I have a great aversion to green peppers. All other peppers are safe, but I HATE green peppers. Speaking of loathing, I HATE peas too, unless they're in fried rice or sparsely in vegetable soup, but sparsely. I've never liked chocolate cake, and I think I've had people not like me for this alone. I was almost booed off the stage at my kids' school when I said this out loud. I have a heavy salt hand.

When my cardiologist said I was his only type of patient that he requires to eat a lot of salt, I was elated.

I love the smell of a skunk. Love it! When we pass the faint smell of a skunk on the road, Jason always turns to me and says, "Do you smell that little hug from Jesus?" I wear patchouli, which would help make the skunk part make sense, right? Given the choice I would pick mountains over the ocean. Still, I love how small I feel looking at the vast ocean.

As I'm sure you've noticed, I'm a kisser. I love to kiss my people. I love a good smooch, but I'm just as fond of a hug or a long snuggle. All my kids are generous with their affection. Little bits of kisses and hugs and loves all day long.

I love to dance. I could be exhausted, in pain, past myself, and I will refuse to get off the dance floor. It is one of my most favorite things to do. And I love to plan a dance party, love it! I love watching my kids dance, and I love to dance with them. I love the face Jason makes when he joins me dancing. He's a mix of happy and when-will-this-be-over? I will look for any reason to have a dance party. That's one of my favorite parts of a wedding.

I think salad, all salad actually, tastes better when someone else makes it. I can build a lovely salad, but if someone else wants to, I say go for it. Speaking of salads, the smell of bacon reminds me of my grandma. She was my hero.

I do not mind what my kids wear. They can steal from my closet, wear socks of opposing neon colors, even leave their hair sticking straight up. I don't care. I do micromanage teeth brushing and bedtime, but beyond that I'm open. We require fruit for snacking. We ask all our kids to take a thank-you bite of everything. That bite says, *Thank you for the effort you took in making me this.* But we do not require our kids to clean their plates. Dessert does come on occasion, but only to those who ate well.

My favorite color is green. I've always wanted to wear fancy boots like the Pioneer Woman. I would love to drive an old Chevy truck, the kind with the wood slats in the back. And don't get me started on fire. I love, love, love fire. I would never be satisfied with logs where the flames are always the same. I want burning, popping, roaring fire.

I like public speaking. It makes me incredibly nervous. But I weirdly like nervous. It's like the nervous before a first kiss. The last time I spoke at the kids' school, I asked for a microphone. They gave me one with a cord. I had way more fun with that than I should have. I thought I was Bob

Barker, walking and swinging that cord. And I told a lot more jokes than expected.

If you live long with an illness, you can begin to be defined by it. I have cancer, but that's only a part of who I am. The bigger reality is that I am Kara. Sometimes I feel like I'm that Kris Kristofferson line—"a walking contradiction." And I like that. I like that a lot.

38

Monday and Wednesday

Monday came, and the news wasn't encouraging. They found that the cancer has metastasized in my brain. My brain. I sat in the corner of my room and cried. Jason and I went for a short walk. And we both cried. Then we picked up the kids. *The kids.* How will I tell them it's in my brain? As Jason and I walked earlier, we decided to tell the kids, just tell them it's in my brain. My brain.

Jason is struggling. We continue to find tumors. Yesterday he looked sweetly at me, and we then talked about doing the next thing, about how we both must faithfully walk into what's ahead of us. Wednesday came and we sent the kids to school and we headed to yet another doctor's appointment.

I didn't want to go. I didn't want to do the next thing. I was scared. I walked into the radiation unit with cancer in my brain. My brain.

We went to the appointment discouraged but left hopeful. Though they didn't talk about a great deal of time being added to my life, they did say they had hope. And they were ready to move quickly as my tumor is still small. I was whisked back to a CAT scan, and the shaping of a mask for the treatment of my brain. My brain.

I never wanted to say out loud that there is cancer in my brain. That's just terrible. But this is now another wrinkle in my story. My story.

39

Leaving on a Jet Plane

We hopped on a jet plane bound for San Diego. We had decided to run away and visit family there and have some time with our little ones. When we heard that the cancer had returned so quickly, the decision for "time away" was easy. Time away spent relishing our moments together. Time away trying to exhale. Time away trying to capture memories. Time away simply to rest.

Cancer brings an intensity to life, a hyperliving that doesn't feel realistic. So we went and put our feet in the ocean, and I wondered if we would remember that. Ella and I sat in the sand and talked about how big God is, but also about how personal He is, and I wondered if she would remember that. I woke my kids up from naps with snuggles and peanut-butter cups, and I wondered about that too.

I realize it all sounds quite self-focused. It is. And it's exhausting. It's not so much that I want my children to remember me, as I want to be woven into the fabric of their living. That's sorta the same thing, isn't it? I want to be present now, alive now, and yes, remembered. I get frustrated when I have to nap because that doesn't feel like living; it feels like I'm missing something.

This vacation is such a gift. Tomorrow we plan to eat breakfast out, then swim and rest and surf and rest, and then maybe repeat it all. Doesn't that sound delicious? It takes all my will to choose to meet the joy of each moment and not linger in the fear of when these moments will end. My head is so divided. I long for a break from my cancer-thinking fears so I can just live in the being-alive-next-to-the-people-I-love.

We are making memories, though. At least I remember so far the well-made cups of coffee, the long swims in the pool, our kids beside themselves with joy in the crashing waves, my big girls' attempts at surfing, the waves coming in and going out and coming in again. I think the people I love will remember these things too, and that includes me.

40

The Thrill of Fear

I have always wondered at the thrill of fear. But after experiencing Disneyland for the first time, I now understand. There is something compelling about fear, something about your stomach in knots that keeps you coming back for more. My daughter put it well after she conquered one Disney ride she was afraid of: "Mommy, I feel a little more courageous now that I tried it. Let's go do something else hard." And there it is. We are all desperately afraid of what's hard, but once we face it, it's possible we find a new joy we hadn't known before.

Every night on vacation I've fallen asleep in the exhaustion of a day well spent enjoying this reality with our children. Every morning I wake and remember my story. I'm often

gripped with fear, like I'm on a ride of unbelievable propor-
tions. I embrace my reality, invite Jesus to walk with me, and
I humbly brave the day. I have moments so crushing at times
I want to fall into fierce tears. But once the ride is over, the
day is done, I recount my story and there is a thrill that I did
it (through the strength of Jesus). I'm not saying that cancer
and chemo are rides at a theme park, because they're not. But
there is an exhausted thrill at having braved one more day.

I cried through the parade at Disneyland. The pageantry
was amazing, the colors vivid, the music utterly memorable.
I watched my youngest enraptured, and I watched my oldest
sneaking ever forward from a place of disinterest to amaze-
ment. I cried at the make-believe I know we longed to enjoy,
to embrace, to run away to if only for a day. This was true
for all of us. We wanted to escape our present tension,
our nail-biting story, to swap it for some pixie dust and a
spoonful of sugar. For a little while it all helped our story
go down. California couldn't change our story, but it did
give us moments to exhale and enjoy one another. For this
I am eternally grateful. For this I whisper, "Thank You."

41

Time

Last week a dear friend texted me some hard questions, asking about my heart. She is a warrior friend who bravely asks and then gently and lovingly listens to my answers without judgment. Last week she asked many questions that brought tears. But her last question has stayed with me. It has seemed to grow in my heart, and become a prayer. Her question was this: *What does your heart hunger for?* My answer was one word and a bunch of tears: *time*.

> Time to hold hands.
> Time to hear a heart.
> Time to share my faith.

Time to quiet an upset mind.

Time to see young love.

Time to walk with another who is suffering.

Time to listen.

Time to talk.

Time for playground girlfriends.

Time to giggle.

Time to fall apart.

Time to comfort the sick.

Time for birthdays, weddings,
    anniversaries, good-byes.

Time for coffee next to my man.

Time for wrinkles and gray hair.

Time with young mamas sharing fears.

Time with old mothers sharing wisdom.

Time for puddle jumping and book
    reading.

Time to spend the day cooking something
    slowly and well.

Time to worship and hear my children
    praising.

Time to match socks.

Time to see my daughters' mascaraed faces.

Time to teach manners.

Time for vacation.

Time for heartbreak.

Time to climb mountains.

Time for camping trips and campfires.

Time for inappropriate jokes.

Time for homecomings.

Time for painted nails and bruised knees.

Time to champion Jason's preaching.

Time to meet every new guest in our
community.

Time to share grilled cheese.

Time to walk on the beach.

Time for seester lunches and scrunchie-
nosed laughing.

Time to make a wreath.

Time to see a car die and drive a different
old car.

Time to know Ella, Harper Joy, Lake, and
Story Jane as grown.

Time to see Jason as a grandpa.

Time to see a cure.

Time for hurt and reconciliation.

Time to write a book.

Time to love.

Time to see mercy.

I could keep going on forever. But I know the truth is that I've been given eternity. In that truth I can peacefully and tearfully rest tonight. God has been so very good to me. I will still continue to pray for more time. And each breath is an amen.

42

Come to Me

This beautiful passage from Matthew is always a comfort, always a challenge.

> Come to me, all who labor and are heavy laden, and I will give you rest. Take my yoke upon you, and learn from me, for I am gentle and lowly in heart, and you will find rest for your souls. For my yoke is easy, and my burden is light. (11:28–30)

I will confess these to be verses I highly regard yet do not fully understand. Through my bald, emaciated days, the prayer that rose out of this passage was a two-word para-phrase: "Jesus, help."

Sometimes I struggle with these verses because I want them to mean that my burden is going to be taken away. I want them to mean my friend's niece won't have to go through chemo at the impossibly young age of two. I want them to mean that my friend will be granted passage home with her new son from the Congo. I want them to mean that the damage done to my friend's GI tract from radiation can be healed and food will again have a safe passage. But I'm pretty sure that's not what these verses mean. I'm pretty sure my preferred pictures aren't at all what Jesus meant.

I think these verses are just platitudes when we only look at them through the lens of how we want a prayer answered. It's the idolatry of wanting it our way. I have all too often been guilty of this one. When I receive these verses and my heart is hard, I roll my eyes and dismiss the kindness extended to me. It's ugly, plain and simple. But when I'm soft, looking Jesus in the face, I am helped; I am given eyes to see grace and hear His voice: "Come to Me."

Truly, the most beautiful thing to me is that even in my hardhearted confusion and bitterness, He doesn't turn away.

He extends His gentle heart toward me, and calls me, and loves me. And I find rest for my soul.

Anne Lamott contends there are three prayers: *Help, Thanks, Wow*. I'm beginning to think at some point the two outer ones collapse into the truth of the middle one, the only one really—*Thanks!*

43

Coming to Town

I've made the joke that cancer brings everyone to town. But that's really the truth, and it's a gift. A beautiful gift. My calendar is filling with sweet love from family and friends who are planning a visit. My entire family has not been together in, well, I can't remember when. A few years ago my siblings and I celebrated Thanksgiving together, but the folks didn't come. So I'm looking forward to this.

Since I have been an adult, my Thanksgivings have included friends who are family to me. This year will be no different. We are expecting twenty-six for the holiday, and I can hardly wait. I have so much to do, but instead I'm heading out to get my hair did.* Like they say in Marion, North Carolina, "We are getting our picture made, and I'm tired of not liking my hair."

I made dinner for the next two nights, bought food in preparation for Thursday, and assigned dishes to my local friends. We have also cleaned the house, but it has been the loose-handed cleaning you do when you know your house is about to be destroyed with the joy of a full home, lots of kids, and even more laughter. I'm no perfectionist: we've picked up our underwear, and we've supplied the toilets with extra tissue. We're all set.

It might take cancer to get us all together, but isn't that lovely? It's beautifully redeeming this ugly for my whole family. And cancer will drive the perfection from you, that's for sure. And isn't that lovely too? Nobody remembers perfection, nobody. But everybody remembers hugs and laughter and taking the time to catch up and be loved. We've got nieces and nephews coming who are taller than me, so I'm planning to wear my high-heeled boots all week. I can hardly, hardly wait.

---

* This is Kara's turn of phrase, a "Kara-ism."

44

Quiet

This morning I was quietly remembering. Life with family is beautiful and messy, a mix of amazing and painful. The distance is felt, the conversations never feel long enough, the fondness really never fully shared. I would be lying if I didn't feel all of our guests counting my days, their silent wondering if this was my last season of thanks. In contrast I saw the freedom in their faces, their blissful unawareness of the number of their days. I'm quietly jealous of their living without numbering their moments. My days feel clipped. Am I appreciating them? Am I savoring the right now? Am I loving as big as I possibly can?

This morning as I was quietly remembering, writing thank-you notes, resting from my short cleaning stint, I looked quickly at Facebook. I saw the news of the sudden death of a high school friend's husband. I lost my breath. I felt lame at my compliments of her beautiful furniture makeovers over the years, even a comment that I envied her beautiful top lip. Almost twenty years between us, but there is this odd connection over social media. I know of her, but I do not know her heart. I have imagined her reality for Jason. The day it's all over. The telling of the children, the cold where there once was warmth. I can imagine that, but I cannot know it, cannot know her pain. I am not her. I don't know the quiet love they shared. Really all I know is that Saturday she had him and Sunday he was gone. This living is beautiful and messy. And often when it's messy, it's horribly messy.

Into this beautiful messy, the baby was born—Jesus, Emmanuel, God-with-us. The comfort the incarnate Christ offers me today is His knowing, His presence. He walked harder than I will ever walk or imagine. He faced utter rejection, pain, deception, and a death I cannot fathom. And He did it all for you, for me, for us, for my Facebook friend who had a husband on Saturday but then didn't on Sunday. I don't think that means our lives necessarily look better. But I do believe that means our lives matter, yours, mine, all of us.

45

Reflections

I've never been a big fan of New Year's resolutions. Simply put, I cannot follow rules, especially the ones I create for myself. I'm more about New Year's reflections, thinking back over the past year and looking ahead at directions I can take to be more intentional in my life.

The year 2014 has found me in the midst of a beautiful exhale from treatment. I'm still in the constant cycle of testing and waiting, but I have met the first moments where breaths don't feel counted. A longer horizon has presented itself with one MRI coming back with encouraging news. It feels glorious. But I do not wish to leave the lessons of 2012–13 behind. I long to live with the intention of noticing my moments. In our crazy, busy, go-go-go society it would be easier to fix my sights on a full calendar and forget the hard we have just come out of.

Still, I find myself here at the beginning of 2014 gloriously ABLE—able to go, able to clean and cook and go do things. For that I give thanks. But when I reflect back on the lessons of my treatment and the pace it set for our home, I wonder if all the going is better. What if my strength has been returned so that I can use it a little wiser this time? I love that my strength is back, but the gift of cancer is that I realize my significance is not in my ability to go and do. For years that's where I found my identity. People were always lining up to consume what I had to offer. My hope for 2014 is that I would be slow enough and quiet enough to hear His voice, to be still and know that He is God and I am not.

46

Quirks

I have never made any bones about the fact that I struggle with home keeping. I have spurts of success followed by moments of utter failure. I have seasons where I'm really great at inspiring the kids to take ownership and participate, and seasons where I just do it and forgo training my children. I have seasons where I love serving my family with laundry love, and seasons where I forget we need clean clothes.

Jason and I have a few small signals that gently remind me that I need to get a few tasks done. They are slight prods to remind me, inspire, and keep me going. I admit they're quite quirky. Around the issue of laundry, Jason has a pair of undergarments he wears that indicate he's out of underwear. I won't go into details, but when I see them, I know it's laundry love time. No words are exchanged, no frustrating pleas for the washing machine, nothing like that. It's just one distinct pair of undies that gets my attention, that pair that I know he would not put on unless he had no other choice. I'm not sure when this started, but it has been an effective way to motivate me to clear a little of my schedule and focus on the house. This little quirky trick has saved us many sensitive talks. I'm super-sensitive to feeling like a failure in this area, so Jason's willingness to wear "that pair" is a true grace.

Another quirk has to do with fresh flowers. It also has to do with home keeping, but let's say it has more to do with flowers, okay? Early in our marriage I clued Jason in to the fact that fresh flowers are the best motivation for me to keep a tidy home. They don't have to be fancy; it's just something about flowers that encourage me to want to keep the house clean. So, as you can see, between things like fresh flowers and "that pair" of undies, we're able to keep at this dance called marriage.

One of my friends calls the marriage of a man and woman the holiest dang thing on earth. I agree, 100 percent. Figure out what it takes, flowers, ratty indicator underwear, whatever. It's worth it, every dang bit.

47

No Awards Yesterday

I did not win any parenting awards yesterday. I'm not sure what the opposite of a parenting award would be, but whatever that is, that's what I would have earned. What is it about parenting that exposes every bit of selfishness in my heart? Every crumb of self-focus I have in my life is exposed through parenting.

In my best move to date, I decided, just decided we were done being sick in our house. I had grown weary of the lingering sickness, so I simply declared us all well. I turned on the music and started cooking dinner. I had a speaking engagement the next day and Jason had meetings to attend, so I decided the most important thing would be everyone being healthy.

My kind and gentle man went upstairs to check on our puny one. He came down to report that our sweet girl still had a fever, plus now an ear infection. Wait, but I declared that we were all well, right? Ugh. Yeah, while my girl was upstairs in need of a caring mama and a soft place to be sick, I was downstairs making no-more-sickness declarations in a complete state of denial. That was yesterday.

Today I woke her sweet face, gave her medicine, loved on her all day long. I promised I would not declare her well too soon. Today I was hers, and I got to tell her how important she is and how much I love her. I brought her water and medicine and kisses. I also brought her an apology, which may have been the most important thing toward her getting well.

I have never been good at caring for sick people. Isn't that ironic? When I've been cared for months upon months and then someone needs me to return the favor and I'm impatient—isn't that the worst? I am making progress in this area, but it's a slow go, and days like yesterday feel like one step forward, four steps back. But days like yesterday remind me of the patience Jesus has with my selfish, impatient heart. And wouldn't you know it, my sweet girl extended the same kind of patience with me. No judgment, no condemnation, just grace, sweet grace.

48

Please!

How do you live well when the living you're
living isn't the living you expected?

Sounds like some kind of riddle, doesn't it? It feels like a riddle I'm lost in every single day. I think this may be THE question most of us are wrestling with if we're honest. I started a new book tonight, a good fiction read. The main character is a grandma, and I was immediately jealous of her. Once she started to complain about her life, I had to put the book down. There I was, reading about a fictional character that I'm dreadfully jealous of, and I found myself absolutely hating her.

I'm thirty-seven years old, desperate to be a grandma someday, and I'm not living the life I expected to be living. I never expected at my young age to be living in the tension of my life soon ending. It's very hard. Suffocating, actually. Jason shared that same suffocating feeling last week. He was at the helm in our house, caring for everyone who was sick, including me. A new despair seemed to enter his heart, one where he felt in a very real way how the life we're living isn't the one we expected.

I want my days to spread out before me without fear of their limit. I want to go on an amazing family vacation in two weeks without the fear that it's my last. I want to not be in the rotation of blood draws, doctor appointments, and scary snorts. I want the old gluttonous days before me that felt like they had no end, when a headache was just a headache and not the return of more cancer.

Tonight I read an article in the *Huff Post* that was my undoing. The author was a young mom writing about living her life without her mama by her side for navigation. It was beautiful, and awful. I don't want that to be the story for my daughters. I don't want them to navigate the hard of this life without a mama, without me. And yet.

These are the desperate hours of faith. Those clawing, begging, gut-wrenching ticks of the clock where the prayers get bone honest: "Please, show me the redemption of this story. Please reveal Your goodness in this hard. Jesus, help me see You."

So I'm living a life I didn't expect, living in the unexpected tension of an unknown future. We all are, aren't we? In our many different ways, we're all living in the desperation of life that hasn't turned out like we'd planned. My unexpected turn is cancer. For others it's singleness, unemployment, a disappointing marriage, broken friendships, and the list unfortunately goes on and on. These desperate, raw, painful turns leave us longing for more, hopefully looking to and for Jesus. "Please, help us see You."

49

I'm Needy

I can't escape it—I'm needy. Everyone around me is needy too. I've got a friend who is headed for exploratory surgery while another friend is flying to the bedside of her dying mama. Neediness is everywhere.

Last week was an unbelievably humbling week where the strength I thought had returned faded into the abyss of yuck. I was once again brought beautifully low, and saw clearly my need. Today I went to the oncologist and frankly discussed my future, how my treatment plan will go forward, and the remaining treatment options available to me. He is pleased with my current treatment and feels it is actually reversing some of the cancer. Two places that previously showed cancer now look to be clear. Still, he said I would probably not have surgery options in the future, that my fighting will be with hormone suppressants, radiation, and … chemo. A trio of hard. That wasn't exactly what I wanted to hear, but I needed to hear it.

After my appointment, I was to meet Jason at a local coffee shop. I was sitting in my car, waiting for him to arrive, when a man came around the corner and sat at one of the outside tables. He looked at me, shrugged his shoulders, and reached in his coat for a giant bottle of whiskey. He drank deeply, then returned to his coffee. His face was tired, his clothes were torn and worn, and I knew this man. I didn't know his name, we'd never met, but I knew him and I believe he knew me, both of us taking different steps down the path of brokenness.

Life can be so hard and the journey toward redemption sometimes feels so long. My peace is often robbed, and I forget to rest in Christ. So I need reminding, I need the truth placed constantly before me. Like the torn and worn man finding his comfort in a bottle, I drink mine with busyness, people, food, endless amounts of stuff to ease the common ache. Brennan Manning knew about this and wrote:

> Getting honest with ourselves does not make us unacceptable to God. It does not distance us from God, but draws us to Him—as nothing else can—and opens us anew to the flow of grace. While Jesus calls each of us to a more perfect life, we cannot achieve it on our own. To be alive is to be broken; to be broken is to stand in need of grace. It is only through grace that any of us could dare to hope that we could become more like Christ.

I'm needy, and that drives me to grace. This brokenness keeps me in a place of waiting at the feet of the One who gives love. In my weakness I travel many roads looking for the comfort only Jesus can provide. Roads of anger, gluttony, laziness, selfishness, control—they all leave me wanting, they all leave me void of real peace. I'd love to tell you these roads are overgrown due to my avoidance of them, but they're not. They are well-worn, well-walked paths in my life.

I will keep looking for grace. But I need help in the journey. I need community and the gentle care of those who know my heart. I need to be shepherded away from the creature comforts I seek that leave me empty. Life is too hard to do alone. And I'm so needy.

50

Craving Grace

Author and speaker Ruthie Delk came to our church last Monday evening to speak to the women. Her words were a much-needed reminder of grace. Ruthie is kind, transparent, and very honest about living in the hard tensions of each day. Her book *Craving Grace* is a study on the simplicity and complexity of grace.

She shared two illustrations that undid me. She shared of two women, one in the midst of great suffering and the other in the midst of great blessing. Both women face the same struggle—trust. One fails to trust that in the deep sorrow over the loss of her husband she can learn to walk in faith and grace as a widow. The other woman is struggling with receiving the blessings of God, wrestling with what to do with God's favor.

Ruthie admitted to us that she is the second woman. God is blessing her words, using her message to teach women of the grace and mercy of God, and she is struggling to trust where it all will lead. Her deepest fear is that she'll enjoy it too much and it will all be taken away.

I actually feel like both women. I'm struggling with my diagnosis, my weakness, and my story. I'm also struggling with the blessings and joy that are coming to us. We have been so lavishly loved and cared for, with exciting opportunities for me to share my story and write a book. And I'm struggling to trust that Jesus is enough for all of it, for the pain and the pleasure, for the joy and the sorrow, for the peace and the devastation. I'm craving a big grace, the kind that is truly sufficient, the kind that covers it all.

ACT THREE

It's better to burn out than to fade away.

—Neil Young, "Hey Hey, My My (Into the Black)"

51

The Hardest Peace*

I'm so excited to share with you the title of my October-releasing book. We are still working on the cover, the subtitle, and endless amounts of other exciting details, but the title is set. So without further ado—*The Hardest Peace*. That's the title of the book that will bear my name with the content holding my heart, my story, my journey, and the invitation to join me and look at your own story.

My editor was sitting with his wife one evening discussing my story. She turned to him and said, "The hardest piece

* **Editor's note:** This entry was taken from an article posted on Kara's blog in February 2014. Her book *The Hardest Peace* released in October 2014, and it is available in print and digital editions.

for me is Kara's children." That first phrase struck him as a possible title, with a slight change. Although the kids are the hardest piece for me as well, it's ultimately about the journey toward *peace* that is the heart of my writing. And that's the slight spelling change he thought might be a good title.

When he presented the title to me, I knew that was it. From the moment he said it, told me the story behind it, we just knew. It has never been debated, never questioned. I love it! I love the journey toward peace, even in all of the hard.

We all have hard, pain, crushing heartbreak. My book is not some attempt to one-up everyone with my hard story. Pain is pain. I'm inviting everyone to look honestly at their hard, whatever that may be, and invite Jesus to join in and gently use it to refine, redeem, restore, and reassure us of His great love.

So there you go, and now you know—*The Hardest Peace*. It'll be available in all the coolest bookstores, you know. Really.

52

A Little Bit of Paradise

I got to fly away to paradise. Because of the kindnesses of so many people, our family enjoyed a week in Maui. Yes, that's right—Maui. I saw, I tasted, and I collected memories that will last this lifetime, my smiling thoughts for the days I have left. But there's always a serpent in paradise, isn't there? And the serpent always brings a lie.

I struggled with this lie the entire trip. I believe Jason struggled with it too. The lie was that the time was a parenthesis of sorts, connected to our story but also not reflective of our story, like it was something set to the side that we had to protect or keep by not talking about our non-Hawaii lives. We struggled to articulate it, and it may not make perfect sense, but we both felt it. So, near the end of our time in Maui, Jason and I sat in the middle of a mall and wept. We big ugly cried over our journey. We shared our envy of couples simply on vacation. Jason admitted his struggles with my story, my conclusion, the return of my cancer, and the ending that feels ever before us. We grieved at how drastically our story has changed in such a short time. And as we said the truth out loud, our truths began to outshine that lie, or whatever it was that created distance between us even in paradise.

As we stayed with the truth, we gradually felt this beautiful freedom to be broken together. We're both struggling with the thought that I'm coming home to die. It took us a lot of courage to admit that. As we packed our things to prepare for the trip home, that was one of the things we packed as well, this reality of the unknowns that face us coming back from paradise. But they are no longer unspoken unknowns because we brought them out in the open where the grace of God could wash over them like a wave.

53

A Love Story

We hit the ground running from Hawaii. Over the past month our church has exploded with young couples. Each week we met new faces new to marriage, new to the awesomely refining life of two as one. Jason came home so excited after meeting yet another young couple that joined us for worship. It's an important season, a season of life we love walking with, as mentors walked with us so many years ago. Jason is excited to meet these couples in their hard, and to open our house to be a safe place for them to be truly honest.

It is an exciting season of life, but it's also a hard season. I remember wanting to be the very best at marriage. But it didn't take long for me to see how lacking in tools we were to do marriage well. We needed support. But we had to start with humility and ask for help, which meant exposing that we did not have it all together. We needed community to do love well. We needed tools to fight fair. We needed support to change our story from one of selfishness to one of sacrifice, gentle communication, and support.

When we interviewed with Jim Daly on *Focus on the Family*, he asked Jason how he would encourage husbands to do cancer well. In the moment, we felt stumped, sad and struggling to process well in an interview setting. We simply said to live in faith and repentance, which is exactly right. But as we left and discussed the interview, we talked through what actually got us through the last two years. I even emailed the producer to talk about possible edits. What really got us through were the years and years committed to learning to love. The endless hours communicating, being mentored, praying, moving toward one another prickles and all. All those years, that time spent learning to love prepared us for the bottom that is cancer. We simply could not have survived any other way. I can see so clearly how cancer can destroy a marriage. I completely understand. That is why the time you spend now, your healthy efforts in love, matters so much. The investment in love you make today will affect your tomorrows. Suffering will come, I promise. Work at building the foundation so when the storms come, you can stand, together.

54

A Million Little Pieces

Ugh, we only know a little, but what we do know isn't encouraging. My heart is breaking into a million little pieces. I put my head down at dinner and cried. I cried for my children having to watch me enter treatment again. I cried at the unknown, and at my felt weakness to face that chemo room again. I cried as I felt for the first time the sense of the unfairness of it all. I cried because I just wanted everyone to have a break from my story.

Without getting into the specific details of the sneaky kind of cancer I have, I will say it has quickly worked its way around the drugs we have tried. We try a drug for a time and it works, and then it finds its way around the drug to invade a new part of my body. It did it to my uterus. It did it to my brain. And now it has done it to my lymph system behind my heart. My doctor has confidence in our new plan, but we all recognize my cancer will work its way around this aggressive treatment too. We're slowing the cancer—that's how we're fighting it. And when we can't fight it this way, we'll move on to other treatments. One day we will come to the end of options, of other treatments. But that day is not today.

55

Provision

Yesterday I had the morning with my community. We talked, we shared, we confessed struggles and weakness. As we were all taking time to share, I looked down and saw a call coming through. The gentleman was calling about my new medicine. He told me the cost of the first medicine and my heart dropped. It was a weighty amount, but I knew we could handle it. Then he told me about the second medicine. I was silent, and sick, and asked him to please repeat what he said. My doctor is putting me on a new blend of medicine that is aggressive, rare, and new. One month of my medicine is $14,000. You read that right—$14,000. He went on to tell me the portion I was responsible for and I utterly broke.

I returned to the study and could not speak. I was reeling, distracted and dumbfounded. Where would it come from? How could we manage? I felt weary of what my disease was costing our family. I snuck a text to Jason giving him the number. He texted me back, asking if that came with a trip to Hawaii. I left the gathering and got in the car and cried. I called Jason and we decided where to meet for lunch. Then I called my oncologist and left a message: "I just don't know how we can do this." The nurse called me back quickly and said she would look into it.

I met Jason at this new burger place. Evidently they have an amazing veggie burger, but I couldn't taste it. My anxiety stole all the flavor away. Jason, however, enjoyed every bite of his. He seemed to be at peace. He knew it would all work out, that we'd figure it out. He said, "We'll pay any amount to keep you here longer." After lunch we walked and held hands, and he reminded me of his love. He reminded me of all the times we have been carried in unexpected ways. While I was spiraling and struggling, he was trusting and knowing. Jason is always good medicine for me.

As we grabbed a coffee, a call came through. The kind nurse on the other end of the line had news. The drug company was going to cover the huge difference we could not manage in one huge lump sum. They were asking us to pay $25. That's right—$25. I looked at Jason with huge tears in my eyes. He just smiled. The nurse then asked if we could cover the other medicine at $300. I laughed and told her she knew how to make medicine feel like a bargain.

I ended the phone call stunned. I looked over at Jason and asked, "How is your faith so strong?" Here's what he said: "I don't think I have a stronger faith, but I have a stronger memory of God's provision for our family." Then he went on to list time after time when we saw God provide in unmistakable ways. I forget so quickly. That's just one of the millions of reasons God gave me Jason.

56

Strength in Weakness

When you pass through the waters, I will be with you;
and when you pass through the rivers, they will not sweep
over you.... Do not be afraid, for I am with you.

Isaiah 43:2, 5 NIV

Why is God-with-us such a hard concept to embrace? I would say it is strength that keeps God at a distance from us. And when that strength is taken, removed, or shaken, then we beg for God to be God-with-us. Until then, however, we keep Him at a safe distance because we simply don't want to be interrupted, questioned, or asked much of in our daily living. When the hard hits, we want Jesus to be right there.

But once things ease up a bit, we say, "Thank You, Jesus. I've got it from here."

The sovereignty of God in suffering is a kindness to keep us utterly dependent in a way our strength resists. Suffering often comes to the strong and is met with bitter anger. It isn't the suffering that causes the anger so much as the taking of strength. Honestly, in the hardest of my treatment, I was not crying out for the suffering to stop, but more for the strength to return. If I'm totally honest, that is my prayer right now—not for fewer days of suffering but for more days of strength.

We love strength, we pet it, we live for it, and when it is gone, we question the goodness of God. But as I have seen in my own story, the taking of strength is grace, huge grace to draw me to Jesus. And now, as I face a different treatment, a hope of improvement, and a small ability to go and go—how will I use that strength? And when the suffering comes again, will my heart be ready to receive it? I hope to be able to say, "Thank You, Jesus, for entrusting me with this new hard. Help me to be faithful in it. Help me to reflect Your goodness in letting me partner with You in suffering."

57

What I Want Most

We are in the final days of the school year. It is our great privilege to attend their performances, speeches, those special moments for our children. We are delighting in their music, their friends, and their hearts that long to share their accomplishments. I am desperate in the audience, beaming upon the faces of my children. My heart is screaming, "I'm here. Do you see me? I'm here, and I love you."

Last night after all the performances and activity, Jason and I sat at our kitchen table and laughed in a way we haven't laughed in a long time. We giggled over simple moments, and teased in a lighthearted way we haven't known much of recently. Our recent moments have been a stumbling to get through, but last night afforded us the grace of laughter.

Last week I visited my friend who'd had knee surgery. She was struggling, stumbling, and my heart hurt for her. I left and called Jason and cried ugly, jealous tears of wanting to heal from my cancer like she will heal from knee surgery. I'm jealous of the strength she will be returned to after she heals. And in that same moment, I repent of my jealousy. It's ugly. It's hateful. I get to receive my story, and she gets to receive hers. We both get to see breathtaking grace that meets us in our stories, stories that are different. That's the deal.

As I was going to sleep last night, I started to pray through the joy that had filled the day. I was naming the graces and giving thanks for the moments embraced and feeling so very full. As I was praying, it suddenly dawned on me—I'm not asking for more. I have not been praying for more of these days, these moments, these joys. And the reason is I've been afraid to ask. What if I really, really ask and the answer is *no*? Would I crumble? Would I be kept somehow in the despair of *no*? Would I be able to swallow the pill of *no*? But last night I stopped being afraid, and I asked for more, more everything.

And while I do want more, more of everything, what I want most is Jesus. More of Him.

58

What's a Galley?

Yesterday I received an email from the editorial director at my publisher. She said my galleys would be ready today. I responded to her email with a few other questions I had about the book, and then I had to be humble and ask, "What's a galley?" I have tried in this process not to show how unbelievably green I am. But I am. She graciously answered that a galley is a bound copy of the book with a spiral binding. These copies are often sent to people who have agreed to read and hopefully endorse your book with gushing reviews of praise!

From the beginning of this publishing journey, the publisher asked Jason to write the epilogue for the book. It has intimidated him, but he knows the value of sharing his heart. He is a really gifted writer, but it's not something he enjoys doing. I have come into the room and witnessed the tears as he's worked on it, but he's never shared the actual words with me. Jason sent his writing to my editor, and I would occasionally ask if he'd heard anything back from him, but Jason has played this one very close to the vest.

Today, with the newly bound draft of my book on the seat in my car, it suddenly dawned on me that I had the epilogue! I hesitated for a moment with a bit of self-talk: *Maybe I should read this somewhere memorable or romantic. Nah, I can't wait.* I opened to the back of the book and quietly digested his words, his beautiful words. On the eve of our anniversary, I read the epilogue Jason wrote for my book, and it was absolutely the best gift he could have given me. I called him in tears to exclaim how much I loved his words. I could hear the relief in his voice.

Tomorrow we will celebrate our golden anniversary. Well, not really, it's not fifty years. But it is sixteen, and if people can do it for their birthdays, we can do it for our anniversary, our happy sixteenth wedding anniversary!

59

Finding Joy*

* Kara gave this graduation address to the Evangelical Christian Academy (Colorado Springs, Colorado) Class of 2014.

Dearest graduates, your story is beautifully written. Rest in it. God delights in you. He sings over you; He is pleased with the creation that is uniquely you. Don't be afraid to let another know you—I mean really know you. If God really knows you and loves you, then with courage you can let another know you too, the messy, beautiful you.

You have this one life. You have been given love, grace, mercy, forgiveness, and joy—share them, give them away. There is no reason to withhold. Let all that Jesus has poured into you pour right back out. And from the outflow of that love, you can love the hurting world around you.

There will be moments, hard moments when God will be specifically loving your heart in hard ways. He will be there, and He is enough. You have imagined what you want your life to be. I challenge you tonight, that when your life hands you unmet expectations, don't move away from Jesus. Move toward Him, be near to Jesus.

I never expected cancer at this young age. But I do know what I can expect. I can expect His love and nearness to meet me in the hard edges of life. I'm learning, learning that Jesus is enough. It will be a lifelong lesson I'm sure, but one so worth learning.

When we have not lived up to our own dreams or when life isn't as we expected it, we struggle with feeling like we've wasted our lives or that we are living without purpose. Often God uses these painful edges of life to draw us into a deeper, richer relationship with Him.

His nearness is enough—it has to be. Let the nearness of God give you courage to face life. And when His nearness doesn't seem near, let those around you remind you. Community matters; your life was meant to be lived with others.

Tonight I want you all to know that your life matters, your words matter, you are not a mistake, there is a lovely plan for your life, and we are so thankful for the years you have already been given. Thank you for letting us be a witness to your life.

So, graduates, walk across this stage tonight and step into the next season of life with the promise of God's nearness going with you. And tonight, I'm praying that Jesus would give you eyes to see the very best of life that will meet you in grace. Not only the future graduations from college, marriage, and future children or careers. But grace in the small, beautiful moments:

> giggles with friends,
> a hike on a fall day,
> a hot cup of coffee,
> a great bargain,
> a view of a beautiful mountain,
> a movie that touches your heart,
> a dinner shared around a table with
>   people who love you.

The big moments matter, and they do await you, but the brilliant part of your story is awaiting you on the boring, mundane days sitting beside a fire on a rainy day. Jesus will be there for all of it. He brings the big graces as well as the little ones. And what cancer has taught me is that the small graces today as well as the big ones tomorrow are the essence of living in faith.

Today is a giant grace day. You have made it through high school. We join you in celebrating this moment. The rest of your brilliant story awaits you.

60

Choices

Always choices meet us in our daily living. I have often talked to friends of the pull of the darkened room where I am tempted to spend endless hours facing a screen, checked out of living. The pull is not a light one but a strong, desperate pull to stop. To quit. Most evenings are like this, a battle for peace before sleep. I've written about my going, going, going, and the honest truth is that my going is directly related to my fear of stopping, stopping and never getting going again. If I slow down, I might hear the depth of my sadness and it might be too much for me.

I am currently dealing with pain. Not little pain, but awful pain. I have lived with pain for so long now that I forget what it's like not to have it. My pain indicates that a tumor is pushing hard against something, or maybe even a new tumor presenting a whole new scenario for me. So there's the physical pain, and the peace-stealing mental pain. My mouth sores have returned, but I simply cannot talk about them. My medicine isn't working, my cancer has spread to my bones, the horizon of my days is growing more limited. My thoughts run rampant, and my fears are enormous and terrible. So I go, go, go, planning my days full to the brim, and I embrace joy where I can: sunshine, girlfriends, the park, a run with my children, listening to Billie Holiday, chopping dinner vegetables.

As my days progress, people ask. Driving to the library, I returned a call to my seester—my favorite, the one who has full access. We laugh, we remember, we share our going. Then she asks. She asks real questions, and my mood darkens. Not a little dark, but deeply dark. I give her short answers that reflect my fears. I tell her the dates of my tests. My endless bleeping tests. And that's about it. I know it's unfair not to give details, but I'm so sick of details. Illness is an absolute beast. A bleeping, bleeping beast! The constant focus on me, the constant waiting for answers. The brave ask the questions and get my dark mood in return. Even my love, my closest love, asks and he gets the dark too. I can hardly escape it. My dear seester sends a text after our call: "I'm sorry. I love you. I know you don't want to talk about it." Those were the words on the screen, but what I heard was, "I hear your ugly voice, but I'm not going anywhere, Kara. I love you."

Unconditional love. Love regardless of the conditions, the circumstances, the darkness. That's the kind of love that keeps me in the battle to live honestly, to live kindly, to live in pain but also to push past it. People like my seester are being Jesus to me; they are choosing to stay and walk with me in the darkness, ugly voice and all.

61

My Role

The news today was bleak. We left without words. Nothing pointed us to hope. I shattered in the car. I called my seester and she shattered. I sent desperate texts to friends. Everything felt broken and undone.

As I quieted down in the bath, I reflected on the role of "keeper" that I have been entrusted with as a mama. We mamas are the keepers of memories. We are the ones to treasure the speech impediments, we are the ones to know the victory of a difficult math concept finally captured, we are the ones who know when to bypass broccoli and pull out the ice cream.

I grieve that my story is taking that role away from me. And I struggle that my babies won't know what a gift the collecting of those memories has been. That's why I write, and write, and write. Because I want them to know how important they are, and how beautiful the small moments of their lives truly are. So I sit and remember and write. I am a keeper.

My babies saw me come home streaked with tears today. They quieted as they listened to the hard in my story. Their faces saddened, but we all promised to enjoy right now. Harper was the first to find laughter. Ella tried to quietly avoid the pain, while Story crawled into my lap. Lake and Jason went to clean the car. We all have our roles and places in this story. I am the keeper.

62

Scary Snort

The call came that my next meeting with the scary snort was approved. I call all scanning machines (MRI, PET, CAT) "scary snorts." That line comes from P. D. Eastman's book *Are You My Mother?* The insurance had initially denied it, but my MRI had indicated that the cancer has grown and is pressing upon my spine.

From my latest test we know a few things. My cancer has grown but it is not in my spine. My chemo is not working. My pain is increasing daily. Our hope is that the cancer's growth is confined to my five lymph nodes. The goal with metastatic cancer (my kind) is to slow the beast. But we struggle to find out how to do this. Tomorrow I will be injected with radioactive sugar. This stuff is so dangerous and toxic that it is stored in lead containers until it is put in my arm. Once it's injected it will tell us where my cancer has traveled. The old places will be measured and compared with the new places. Hopefully there won't be new places. That's my prayer.

So tomorrow's scary snort (PET scan) will be faced with Jesus and Jason at my side, and a peace within me. I love and hate these things. They tell us what we need to know, and what I wish we never had to know. Regardless of the news, I am not alone. Scary snorts are not the boss of me.

63

New Borders

I will bless the LORD at all times; his praise
shall continually be in my mouth.

Psalm 34:1

What does it mean to bless the Lord at all times? What does a life of constant praise look like? How do I turn toward Jesus in my desperation and not simply turn away in fear and anguish? How do I trust when the story continues to crumble my hopes and dreams? I often feel like the boy's father in Mark 9[:24]: "I believe; help my unbelief!"

The test results came in from my PET scan. The cancer has found new borders to invade, new places to overtake. I am struggling with nerve pain. Nights have been the hardest. Because of the recent pain we were not surprised by the results, not caught off guard. But that kind of news still breaks us further.

I have been offered a new plan, new pills, a new angle of attack to slow this beast. I will dutifully take my pills and attempt to manage the painful side effects. I hope it will slow this cancer. I hope it will even destroy it. I still have those kinds of hopes. But I feel like I'm fading, you know like in *Star Trek* when someone is being beamed away? That's how I feel, like I'm becoming a different arrangement of myself.

So how do I bless the Lord when I'm being beamed away? One breath at a time. That's one of the lessons cancer has taught me, that today is all I have, and I must keep my eyes focused on what's in front of me, and do the next thing in love. I have faces to kiss and bags to pack and prayers to pray and love to share right now, right here, today. And so I say "Thank You" for these things while also swallowing the new pills that hopefully can keep more cancer armies from crossing my borders. Blessing the Lord is not clean; it's not just when things are easy and good and healthy. It's thanking Him at ALL times and in ALL circumstances, not for the painful things but for His presence. Jason says that's what peace is, and I believe him.

I've seen a blessing-the-Lord-at-all-times that comes via a painted-on smile. It's fake and I believe people can smell that a mile away. The real blessing-the-Lord comes via wearied brows above exhausted eyes and tearstained cheeks. But beneath it all His praise is still in our mouths.

64

The LORD

My soul makes its boast in the LORD;
let the humble hear and be glad.
Oh, magnify the LORD with me,
and let us exalt his name together!

Psalm 34:2–3

In Scripture, when you see the word "Lord" written in all caps, it is referring to Yahweh. It is the name that says God is unchangeable, the God who is with you and me always and forever, the God who is the sustainer of our souls, the God who keeps His promises, the God who is good. And all of my life depends on that goodness, even in the midst of my hard.

The LORD—this means He is trustworthy and the humble can rejoice because He is who He says He is. It means when my story doesn't follow the script I had hoped for, I can still walk in faith, knowing my life, my moments, and even my pain are not mistakes. I can magnify the LORD who does not look upon my story with indifference. In my humbled state I can boast in the fact that I am held and kept by the faithful hands of God. There is not a rogue molecule in my body that is beyond the knowing of God.

Jesus cared about the deeply broken. He met them, loved them, healed them, and walked with them. And He does the same with you and me. There is no despair that the LORD cannot reach and infuse with peace. It is not a peace like the world gives, one that is here today and gone tomorrow. The LORD's peace is enduring, one that makes the humble *glad*!

65

Latigo Ranch

Jesus loved our family bigger than we ever could have imagined when someone made this once-in-a-lifetime trip possible for us. We had no idea when we said *yes* what a huge grace it would be to our family. Months ago when the opportunity came to us, Jason and I saw it as a gift to our children. What we didn't know then was how much of a gift it would be to us as well.

We didn't know months ago what the week before this trip would hold. We did not know it would hold crushing news, new treatment, continued heartbreak. There was no way we could have known. My oncologist was nervous to start a new treatment with me so far away from him, but he also knew I needed to grab life while the grabbing was possible. So we bought cowboy boots at the thrift store and blew out of town.

Latigo Ranch is a sanctuary of gentle, quiet grace. Just what we needed, all of us. I have never cried leaving a vacation, even Maui, like I cried leaving Latigo. The kids were deeply loved, as were we. I told the owners that their ranch had restored us in ways we thought might never be restored. I realize that sounds dramatic, but it's the truth.

Latigo understands that children need to get dirty. Latigo also understands that parents need a little time to themselves. And they put all this under the heading of REST. So you can rest riding a horse? You bet your boots you can. The kitchen staff, the wranglers, the maintenance guys, the owners, they all understand this and go the extra mile to make sure the week is rest-full. Latigo is a "dude ranch," which means you show up there and so do other people, also known as strangers. On Sunday afternoon, twenty-seven of us met for the first time. By the following Saturday afternoon, we all parted as dear friends. I have to tell about two of these people, I just have to.

66

Jo and John

She was beautiful in every sense of the word. She was gentle and soft toward her children, and she loved her man (John) so big. Her name was Jo. One evening Jo and John and Jason and I found ourselves at the dinner table. We shared our story and they shared theirs. They too have wrestled cancer's many painful blows. John was the one who fought cancer nearly five years ago. They were refined and made beautiful through their pain-filled journey. I couldn't get enough of them.

After one dinner where the four of us were with another couple, all of us telling our stories, I stood and apologized for bringing tears to the new couple. Outside afterward Jo and John pulled me aside and gently admonished me: "Kara, never apologize for bringing something real and meaningful to a conversation. The world is filled with shallowness. Be fearless in sharing your story with another. Don't ever apologize."

After our last lunch on our last day, everyone was saying good-bye to new friends and the amazing staff of Latigo. Many were talking about making plans to "come back next year." Jo followed me out on the front porch, noticing I was fighting to be brave. She said, "Kara, I know you are hurting hearing everyone talking about coming back next year when you don't know if you'll have a next year." Then she wrapped me in a hug and let me cry. My tears were safe with Jo, she understood, she was a safe place for me to fall. In fact, she'd been that for me all week long. As had Latigo Ranch.

67

July 14

Tomorrow is my birthday, the day I came to be a part of this beautiful world. This past week I have thought much on this simple day, and I've found myself in tears. I'm not exactly sure where all the tears have come from, but I'm going to try to write it out.

You see, my journey is intertwined with my birthday. It was two years ago this weekend that I found my cancer. My diagnosis was confirmed on July 23, but I found my cancer in the shower just before my birthday. So in a very real sense my birthday is a marker of my struggle these last two years, a struggle to live each and every day in the valley of the shadow of cancer.

When we started this battle, Story felt like a baby. When we started, we didn't know if we would even have these two years. They have been hard beyond belief. This battle has chipped away at Jason's beautiful optimism. He has seen what no one else has, and it's taken a toll. Still, we are grateful beyond words to have had these two years. We wouldn't trade them for anything, for they have been full of big, giant Jesus love like we'd never experienced before.

Tonight I go to bed looking forward to the little faces that will meet me in the morning to kiss me and feed me something they've proudly created. They will want to celebrate me, their mama—me, Kara Tippetts. Tomorrow I will turn thirty-eight, and I can't wait to be older. I'd love the gift of a gray hair or maybe a new wrinkle. That sounds silly, right? But if there's ever a day to be silly, it's your birthday. Happy birthday to me.

68

Jesus Knows

Lake was struggling. Struggling with me, struggling in general. Everything was disappointing his heart. We were wrestling with the edges of each other. We have gone a long season without feeling the edges this deeply. He was angry, angry in a way that tears won't stop, a mix of not getting what he wanted from me plus something else. I could hear the something else, but I couldn't name it.

I asked the girls to go make lunch while I talked with Lake. I asked him to look at me, and immediately he softened and his voice became small. With tears in his eyes he told me I haven't been very much fun lately. He said I'm in my bed a lot. And he was feeling angry about it. Of course the first response deep in my mama heart was, "I'll do better! I'll fight harder!" But I knew those were lies. Things are different now. The go-go-go mama that Lake knew and remembers has slowed down in a way that has hurt the heart of my amazing little boy.

What's a mama to do in such a moment? I simply said, "Lake, I'm sorry." I told him I was sorry his mama has cancer. I told him I'm sorry for the ways that is making his heart sad. Though I wanted desperately to make it all better for him, I couldn't. This is an area where Lake will have to find his steps. I believe in my weakness, Jesus will teach him strength. Where I am less, Jesus will be more. I cannot fix this, but Jesus can handle this. Jesus knows.

I took Lake's dirt-stained hands in mine and prayed. I prayed for strength beyond myself. I prayed for Lake to meet his disappointments with a gentle heart. I prayed for both of our angry selves and asked Jesus to help us love one another well when we feel that anger. I am not disappointed in his anger. It is inevitable. More importantly, it is honest. But I believe there is a story bigger than our anger. I believe we must feel it, certainly not deny it, but

we also must not hold on to it. My dear children are having to grow up too fast in certain ways. In certain ways,
so am I. And while we don't always know what to do or
what to say or even how to feel, Jesus knows.

69

The Tears in My Popcorn

Some friends and I saw the movie *The Fault in Our Stars*. When I left, I simply didn't feel Ella was quite ready for it. Months passed and one evening we were having dinner with friends when one of those friends, Chris, gently spoke to me about my decision to keep Ella from this book and movie. He was so kind to listen to me and my fears. Then he said something I had not considered. Chris has a unique perspective because he lost his mama at a young age to cancer. He said, "Kara, Ella is the only person among her peers that understands the pain of cancer. Letting her read this book and see this movie will help her not feel so alone." Sometimes you hear someone say something and you just know they're right. I felt that way when Chris spoke to me.

I told Ella she could read the book, and she consumed it. The movie had released months ago and was now at the dollar theater, so we ran away last night to watch this heart-breaking story. On the way, we talked about the sex scene in the movie. I told her how Jason and I deal with scenes we don't feel comfortable watching. She heard my heart in it, and I believe she was careful to protect her heart when the scene approached. There was a point in the movie where Hazel Grace bowed her head and said, "This is not the life I want." That line cracked the brave veneer of my daughter, and she broke.

Together we left the movie arm in arm. We sat quietly in the car and shared our hearts, our hurts, and the pain of the present. I was able to tell her what a cherished child she is. I was able to articulate through my tears my hopes for her story. I shared that if I do fly away, I'd like for her to let my girlfriends step in and bring mama love to our family. But we were honest about the high calling of being the oldest in a family like ours. I went on to ask her to enjoy life, even if my life is fading. I asked her to embrace joy, to live each moment bravely. Then we wept, wept for the story we have been asked to receive and struggle to understand. Then we spoke of the hope of heaven, a hope lacking in the movie.

Another of the lines in the movie is "That's the thing about pain. It demands to be felt." Goodness, I believe that to be true. Chris was right, the book and movie were good for our hearts. All of us try to live tough, braving the pain. Sometimes we need moments side by side in a dollar theater to let go of the pressure that builds up over time, to just pull the release valve and let the tears flow.

70

Harper Full of Joy

Three years ago I went on a "ten year" trip with Ella. The goal was to have fun, connect, discuss coming adolescence, and share faith. Together we looked at the book *The Care and Keeping of You*. American Girl puts out this book, and it is really a lovely creation about body changes and speaks well of caring for yourself. I also explained sex to Ella on this trip. I told her that her friends would try to tell her things about sex, but I hoped she would trust Jason and me with her questions.

We also spent some time discussing the middle school temptation to listen to peer voices more than parent voices. I told her this was natural, but I still hoped she would listen to us. And last, I had asked her friends to write her letters, prayers, hopes, stories. They were amazing. So many challenged Ella to take hold of her faith personally and walk her own path to Jesus. In some ways Ella was too young to take all that in, but I've saved the letters for her. She'll cherish them one of these days.

But now it's Harper's turn for the "ten year" trip. We'll follow the same outline as Ella's, but Harper and Ella are very different. I'm customizing the trip specifically for Harper. For instance, Harper doesn't care much for food. She's like her daddy in that she simply eats for fuel to get going, not for the nuances of taste in every bite. So finding the perfect food spot won't be on our list. But Harper loves art, so we plan to look at beautiful art and hopefully even make some together. Harper also loves to play, so we'll play in the pool, play in the hotel, play as we shop. And Harper loves to talk, so we'll spend most of our time loving each other with words. It's the place where Harper and I connect.

Harper is like me in that she can get a bit fixated on something. Currently she is fixated on purchasing a rodent of some type for a pet, so I'm sure a lot of our conversation will revolve around that. So we're going to run away together, just me and Harper, and enjoy one another in the big city of Denver. I have letters from her friends as well and we'll read them, like I did with Ella. But Harper is the child who wants to know what's going on, so in addition to rodents, we will also talk about cancer. She is the one who is comforted by the truth. Harper is not afraid to look at the hard and ask real questions of it. And I cannot wait!

71

Dear Cancer …

There are a few things I'd like to say to you this morning. A lot of what I want to say is salty and ugly, but I will do my best to use nice words and not the ones I often drop around my house. Cancer, you are and always have been an unwelcome guest in the home of me. But I thought we could work it out. I thought you'd see how poorly I keep house and you would just leave. But that hasn't happened. You keep leaving your mess all over the place.

You have introduced me to so many kind faces that have worked gently to ask you to leave the house of me. They've all told me to fight you, but I hate to fight; it just isn't how I'm made. You have left corners of me broken that will never again be the same. Just yesterday I heard of all the scar tissue you've left in my lungs. I feel that damage as I wheeze through bedtime kisses. You, cancer, are a jerk-faced ninny muggins that just won't leave. I'm beginning to despair that you'll never go.

I'm not sure of the right attitude to have toward you. I want to weep one moment and I want to live bigger than I've ever lived before the next. Before you I lived comfortable. If I didn't feel good, say a muscle strain or something, I'd take it easy, not do anything. But now, with you, I'm learning my feelings have little to do with living or not living.

So here we are. The truth is that now you are in my bones, my bone marrow, my blood-making place. I did not want you there. I asked you not to go there. But you did it anyway. But here's something. You will never separate me from the Holy Spirit. He's watching you, every single cell of you. He's the One giving me all this peace that confounds you. You won't take my joy, cancer. You won't keep me from living as close as I can to my people. And I know you think you are killing me with all your fast-growing cell business, but you are not the boss. The day I breathe my last is exactly numbered. You don't have a say in that, sorry. And when that day comes, and it will come, my people will be kept safe in God's beautiful arms.

I'm tempted now to slip into that salty language, so I'll stop. I do hate you, and I'm still here.

Kara

72

Five Thoughts on Dying Well

That'll really brighten your day, huh? Honestly, though, I think about this all the time. How does one die well? How does one glorify God in death? Here's what I've come up with for today. I'm sure as time passes I could expand on this list, but this is enough for today.

1. Live with deep forgiveness to share and honest repentance with those you love. Keep short accounts and don't find offenses that aren't there. I often share with my children the story of Steven,

a young boy in my elementary school. I treated him poorly—no friendship, no gentleness, no kindness. The hard of cancer caused me to track down Steven and ask for his forgiveness. He gently extended mercy and forgave me. He offered kindness I did not deserve.

2. Try to live each day intentionally. It's hard, and I often fail and fall into lazy mode. But I try to spend my days looking deeply into the eyes and lives of those I love. I stare. I smile. I do my best to remember to laugh. Even with all the hard in my life, it's still a wonderful life that deserves our attention.

3. The time I spent in the past leaning on and learning of God serves me well now. It was time well spent. Don't neglect your heart and your faith in seasons where all is well. The seasons

will change and you'll be glad for the foundation you have.

4. Don't squander a moment. I understand small talk, but I'm now at the point where I believe small talk is for small people, and God wants us to live big. Ask the hard questions, have the deep conversations, contribute to what's meaningful and real about life. The pretend story is not really a story at all.

5. Reach out. I regret the comfort I kept myself isolated in for so many years. God has lavished His undying love on us, so why don't we extend ourselves armed with love to our hurting neighbors? Yes, we're selfish. But we can be better than that, we really can. Reach out.

73

Dearest J. K. Rowling …

When I was in college, my dearest friend, Amy, babysat for a professor's family that had an evening ritual called "tiger time." Amy came back to the dorm and told us of the delights of this family. Each evening the children pretended to be baby tigers as they jumped in bed with their mother—the mama tiger—and they would snuggle and read each night. As babysitter, my friend Amy was asked to step in for the mama tiger and perform the honorary task of reading. She loved it.

I remember feeling awed by this intentional love, hopeful that I would one day love my children in a similar way. I started out strong, but I confess that in the struggle of cancer

and busyness we forgot the wonder of reading together in
my bed at night. We still cuddled, but we lost the wonder of
fiction. I felt the age range of my kids was just too impossible
to find a middle ground. I was woefully wrong.

Then I heard that my friend Matt read the entire Harry
Potter series to his little ones. I wondered if I could manage
that alongside the battle for every breath in my body. I turned
to my husband one evening and said, "I think at the end of
my days I will be sad I didn't read more to my children." And
who wants to die sad? Right, so I started with Harry Potter
and the Sorcerer's Stone.

I was still concerned about the age range, but it has
met us in such wonderful ways. My baby rarely makes it
two pages; she's content to snuggle in and fall asleep. But the
others listen close, eager for more of your story. My second
born and I actually had quite the quidditch discussion at
dinner tonight. All that to say it's been wonderful. You have
brought this joy to us—thank you!

Last night we finished the chapter that ended so tenderly,
the one where Harry and Ron accepted Hermione as their
friend: "But from that moment on, Hermione Granger
became their friend. There are some things you can't share

without ending up liking each other, and knocking out a twelve-foot mountain troll is one of them." We loved it. You see, we get it, the hard, and how you have to do it together, and how that glues you. Again, thank you.

A Mama Tiger (Kara)

74

It Is Love

We crowded our table with families that are partnering with us in life, in brokenness, in limping together toward the gospel and looking to our dear Jesus together. We all braved the hard, shared burdens, admitted to the struggles we have faced and by God's amazing grace have come through. We shared the edges and the fog within which we all still stumble. We ended in prayer, and by the amen, my spine and hip were screaming in such pain that I had to leave the room. Tears were coming down and I couldn't stop them.

The kids ran upstairs and quickly readied for bed. Then they came eagerly to my room to hear the end of Harry

Potter. I was grumpy and wrestling with the angry edges of great pain. I looked desperately at them and said I just couldn't do it. I saw the deep disappointment in their faces. But all at once, the pain eased. I don't know why or how, but it did. I called the kids back in, and we all snuggled close and listened to the end of our book. I have to share this part with you. It is stunning. Harry could not understand why he was not destroyed—as a baby, and also as he faced Voldemort. The answer, provided by Albus Dumbledore, reflects my hope and my love.

Dumbledore says, "Your mother died to save you. If there is one thing Voldemort cannot understand, it is love.... To have been loved so deeply, even though the person who loved us is gone, will give us some protection forever. It is in your very skin."

Isn't that beautiful? Love changes us. It changes those we extend our love to. Love matters, always. I know I write a lot about love and kindness. I do that because I need reminding. I can get lost in my own sorrow, my own fears and shame. I can become so consumed with my own story that I forget the other stories around me. Jesus died to save us. And if there's one thing the Enemy of our hearts cannot understand, it is the love of God. It will give us protection, even in the hardest of hard. It is in our very skin.

I'm headed into chemo today. I'm ready to walk in there and fight, fight with all I have, fight for love.

75

Oh What a Night
(Book Launch)

Friday night was a night I will carry with me forever. Forever. I entered a room full of so much love I could not take it in. I struggled to look at the audience because I really couldn't believe all these people had come to hear me and my feeble words. I tried to look at them but just could not. So I looked at the front row where my family and dear friends were seated. I could look there. I could do that.

Having a book published is such a dream come true. When I was approached to write the book, the publisher asked me who else had contacted me about a book contract. My drink almost came out of my nose. Seriously? Who else?

Like no one else, just David C Cook. Jason and I giggled afterward over how I almost choked to death when I was talking about writing a book. But what a gift it has been.

As I was praying about what to share, a very clear thought came to me. In that room full of love, in that room filled with support for our story, our family, and our community, I wanted four little people to hear from their mama. I wanted, in that moment, for those four little people to hear publicly how much their mama cherishes and treasures them. So I decided to read the letters that I wrote to them, letters that are included at the end of *The Hardest Peace*. I thought I could do it, and I guess I did, although I wept through the reading. When I finished, dear Story Jane brought me a tissue. Jason said all the children cried. Jason said he did too. And I treasure those tears. Yes, they are tears of sadness, but they are also tears of knowing that they are fiercely loved children. And that their mama's fierce love comes from an even greater love that will one day meet them, I hope years and years and years from now.

Some have called me heroic, for the fight, for the journey. I'm no hero. I'm just one broken woman looking for grace. I'm one needy heart in need of forgiveness. I'm just like everyone else, fighting to see grace, to live gently, to walk in integrity. It's a daily battle, and some days it's a war. And many days I blow it, bad. But there is always forgiveness.

And this story, it is mine to share. I have to be a witness to the script I've been given. If there's anything beautiful in it, it is because of the Beautiful One—Jesus.

ACT FOUR

End? No, the journey doesn't end here.
Death is just another path, one that we all must take.

—J. R. R. Tolkien, *The Return of the King*

76

Letter to My Readers upon My Death

I just wrote the simple title: "Letter to my readers upon my death," and I'm undone. This is a letter I have written in my head for months, but putting the first words on paper is my undoing. I cannot begin to use this simple language to express the heart of what I feel for this community. There is so much love in this community that I can barely take it all in at times. I have been prayed for, cried over, and my story shared over and over. You all can't know the love I have felt from each of you.

It's impossible for me to not imagine coming to this place again to share my heart anew with you. It seems impossible that this journey has finally come to an end. But I've done gone and flown away to the land of no more tears—won't you rejoice with me? My pain is gone, my fears are calmed, and I'm in the sovereignly good hands of Jesus. He is my forever enough now. What bliss I'm sure I'm enjoying. It's hard for me to separate my feelings for that place and this.

If you have known my heart and met me here, would you commit my family to your prayers? Prayers of knowing the nearness and comfort of God. For the rest of their days, not simply the coming months. Would you commit them to the heart of your praying? I know it's a large ask—but God is big, and I believe you are capable of this kind of big prayer love for my family, my community. I believe God has beautiful things in store for my people, and I'm greatly comforted thinking of all your prayers backing my loves.

I have prayed long and hard about what will come of *Mundane Faithfulness*—this simple place where grace is raised high and Jesus is exulted. Jason and I have decided to keep it going with the special care of two of my friends. My web designer, Jacob, and my Blythe are going to continue sharing these words of grace. They have all my archived writings, and Blythe will be offering her original writings as well as guest posts from my friends. Jason is also planning on sharing—but he may need a little time. I know y'all will be gentle with him. His heart must be unbelievably broken just now. He will find his footing, and y'all must know—you are important to him. He reads your words as diligently as I do.

I don't know how to adequately express thanks to each of you. You have stumbled with me in this journey toward my last breath with such comfort and grace. I'm humbled to have been given such love and care from mostly strangers. It's astounding. Thank you.

If you would like to give a small contribution to our family (a trust for the kids) instead of flowers (though I pray you would feel no obligation), please do so here. The funds will be used for the children. Checks can be made payable to my guy, Jason Tippetts, who will be the steward of the money, at PO Box 49727, Colorado Springs, CO 80949. Contributions are not tax deductible. Please feel no obligation whatsoever. We are so richly loved and kept.

I love you, dear reader. Our time together has been a highlight of my life. You have prayed for me through so many difficult circumstances. So many days you were the grace that showed up. Our family has known such peace as a result of your faithful praying for our family. Thank you. Thank you. Thank you.

77

Something Else

I sent you the link to the rare Mary Oliver
Interview in hopes her wild voice and
Silky words would inspire you to write.
I knew she'd wooed your mind when
You began texting me quote after quote
You'd copied down, this one your
    favorite—
I SAW WHAT LOVE MIGHT
    HAVE DONE
IF WE HAD LOVED IN TIME.
But you never sent the one I hoped
You'd hear and pause to consider—

WHEN THE MORTAL DIES
IT WILL BECOME SOMETHING
    ELSE—
For that is the line the poet spoke that
Made me think of you.

Now that you're gone my grown-up
    thoughts wrestle with
Exactly what that something else
    is that you've become.
While off to the side the faith
    I held as a child
Holds that you're now a part
    of everything from
The warmth of the winter sun to
The unself-conscious laughter
    of children to
The fragrance of lilac blooms in June.
For in death you were swept up into Him
And since He holds all things
    then it's not a stretch

At all to say you're now a part
    of the grand show.
Mary Oliver would say you're
    EVIDENCE OF THE
    CONTINUANCE.
But Kara Tippetts would grin
    wide and say *Oh, Mary,*
After death there is something else.
There is everything else. There is Jesus.

P.S. You'll have to forgive us if we
    have days or weeks where
We are unlikeable in our grief. This is only
    because we liked you so very much.
Death may have lost its sting,
    but it still burns.
And we press on here in the
    strange beauty of sadness.

Bibliography

Delk, Ruthie. *Craving Grace: Experience the Richness of the Gospel.* Chicago: Moody, 2014.

Green, John. *The Fault in Our Stars.* New York: Penguin, 2014.

Lamott, Anne. *Help, Thanks, Wow: The Three Essential Prayers.* New York: Penguin, 2012.

Lloyd-Jones, Sally. *The Jesus Storybook Bible: Every Story Whispers His Name.* Grand Rapids, MI: Zonderkidz, 2007.

Manning, Brennan. *The Ragamuffin Gospel: Good News for the Bedraggled, Beat-Up, and Burnt Out.* Colorado Springs, CO: Multnomah, 2005.

Rowling, J. K. *Harry Potter and the Sorcerer's Stone.* New York: Scholastic, 1998.

Schaefer, Valorie. *The Care and Keeping of You: The Body Book for Girls.* Middleton, WI: Pleasant Company Publications, 1998.

Spurgeon, Charles. *Morning by Morning.* Peabody, MA: Hendrickson, 2006.

"Losing myself in the startling light of Kara's story, I have found who I am, who He is, and more of the meaning of every breath."

Ann Voskamp, *New York Times* bestselling author

finding grace in the everyday

Kara Tippetts knows the mundanity of life as a young mother, the joy of watching her children grow, and the devastating reality of stage-four cancer. In *The Hardest Peace*, she invites us to see the grace of the everyday in all seasons of life and to live well even when living is hard.

transforming lives together

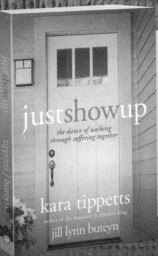